SPOOKS DELUXE

SPOOKS DELUXE

Some excursions into the

SUPERNATURAL

As told to *and recounted by*

DANTON WALKER

Franklin Watts, Inc.
NEW YORK

From Ghoulies and Ghosties
And long-legged Beasties
And Things that go bump in the night—
Kind Lord, deliver us!

(*Scottish. Anonymous.*)

CONTENTS

TO BEGIN WITH—

Sure, I believe in ghosts! *Why not?*

I believe in atomic energy, in television, radio, the telephone, the electric eye and a thousand other man-made miracles that we take for granted today but which a century ago might have been ascribed to witchcraft. I believe in allergies, which at one time *were* ascribed to witchcraft— hay fever was, at any rate—and I believe in animal magnetism, malicious or otherwise, and that indescribable element that makes people fall in love. I believe in life and death, and who is to define them?

Some people are born into the world color-blind, or tone-deaf, or without a sense of smell. Do they think we're crazy because we can see, hear or smell things they can't? I've never seen a ghost and I hope I'll never see one. But plenty of other people have.

I have read a great many stories on the supernatural and nearly every one begins, "No, I don't believe in ghosts, but—" after which the writer proceeds to marshal an array of facts, figures, names and dates proving that he *does* believe in ghosts and hopes you will, too.

However, this book doesn't set out to prove anything. It is intended only as entertainment or, at the most, an "exercise in hypothesis." The stories told herein are true; otherwise there would be no point in printing them. Anyone can "make up" a ghost story, and the tendency in recounting tales of the psychic or supernatural is to enlarge, exaggerate or embellish them in the interest of making a better yarn. Better understatement than overstatement, I maintain, even at the risk of minimizing the drama, color and suspense.

Most of these stories have come to me casually, through contact with professional people of reputation and standing, in the course of interviewing them as a newspaper columnist. I soon blundered onto the fact that nearly every man

9

jack of 'em had *some* experience that might, by a slight stretch of nomenclature, be called a "ghost story," and from then on I made a point of drawing them out on the subject.

No; none of them "believed" in the supernatural, yet each admitted that his experience could only belong in that category—or at least in the realm of the supernormal or unexplainable. In quite a few instances, having told their story, they immediately began to back away from it, declining permission to put it in print for fear that they might be ridiculed. Necessarily, then, many of the case histories are tantalizingly fragmentary and some anonymous, yet all deserve to be included as part of the "evidence."

Some of the experiences would seem to be utterly pointless but none the less valid. For example, Harriet Parsons, Louella Parsons' daughter, told me that she once dreamed of seeing a man riding a bicycle down a street in Los Angeles. She didn't know the man but the dream left a distinct impression on her memory. Three days afterward she *did* see the man riding down the selfsame street in Los Angeles on a bicycle, in the flesh, and immediately recognized him. She didn't know him then, or afterward, and hadn't the slightest idea why she should have seen him in her dream, or in real life. She was quite baffled by the whole experience. And the more you delve into the subject, the more baffling it becomes.

In a superb collection of ghost stories collected by William Stevens, called *Unbidden Guests*, there is an attempt made to break down ghosts into categories, such as "quiet ghosts," "noisy ghosts," "ghosts with a mission," "ghosts who merely come and go," etc.

Haunting by the sense of smell seems to be one of the most familiar methods by which apparitions make their presence felt, and there are hundreds of such incidents on record. One of those cited by William Stevens, a classic example, concerned the Empress Eugénie of France. After the fall of the Third Empire, the Emperor, Empress and their young son Louis took refuge in England. Louis, or "Lou-Lou," as his mother called him, was eventually given a commission in a British regiment and sent to South Africa, where he was killed by the Zulus. This was in 1879. The body was recovered and sent back to England and a stone cairn set up by the river marking the spot where he died. It became an obsession with the Empress to find this spot and she was eventually humored by the British Government and permitted to go to Africa to find it. When the search party arrived, the Empress insisted on fighting her way through undergrowth that deterred even the guides, led on by the strong odor of violets—the scent that her son had favored in his toilet water and shaving lotion. And she found the cairn of stones marking the spot where the young prince had died!

Ghost stories, of course, are as old as time. You'll find them in the Bible and you'll find them in Shakespeare, who probably drew on actual incidents. Libraries everywhere are filled with them. Hereward Carrington (apparently the pen name for Hubert Lavington, a British-born editor and writer who has spent a lifetime investigating or writing about psychic phenomena) has a private library of some seven thousand volumes. Carrington collaborated with Nandor Fodor, a psychoanalyst, on a book titled *Haunted People*, and Fodor's chapter on "The Psychoanalytic Approach to the Problems of Occultism" is probably the first original contribution to the subject in our time.

Tennyson, Ruskin, Gladstone, Thackeray, Sir Walter Scott and Victor Hugo are a few of the famous authors who have concerned themselves with tales of the psychic or supernatural. Edith Wharton, Henry James, Rudyard Kipling and Conan Doyle are some of the more modern writers who have devoted their literary talents to the subject. And Sacheverell Sitwell rather recently turned out a tome on the subject of *poltergeists*, a rather special kind of ghost that is given to haunting people, rather than places.

John Wesley, the founder of Methodism, has many references in his famous diary about apparitions seen by himself and his family, not once but many times. In fact, the haunting of Epworth Rectory, the Wesley family home, is one of the liveliest hauntings in history.

Some students of the occult are inclined to include Joan of Arc's mysterious "voices" in the realm of the supernatural, as indeed they were. It is a matter of history that James IV of Scotland was visited by an apparition that warned him against an invasion of England. James ignored the warning and fell at Flodden Field. Napoleon, while incarcerated at St. Helena, told those about him that he had seen and conversed with the shade of Josephine, who

11

warned him of his approaching end. A more recent dictator who was reputed to have heard "voices" was Hitler. The story goes that he entertained familiars of the spirit world at his solitary mountain retreat at Berchtesgaden—familiars who apparently misled him as badly, and as deliberately, as did the three witches of Macbeth.

Ghosts in wartime are no novelty: there are innumerable instances on record. One of the favorite legends of World War I concerned an apparition of a woman who appeared frequently to Allied soldiers in the Belgian trenches and was known to them as the "Angel of Mons." While on a boat going to Puerto Rico some years ago I was entertained by an army officer's story about an incident that happened during the Spanish Civil War. A Loyalist night surprise raid on a Rebel battery failed, it seems, because the commanding officer believed that he saw a horseman leading troops against his command. It developed later that the soldiers defending the battery were asleep at the time and the attack undoubtedly would have succeeded. The officer was convinced that the mysterious horseman was the ghost of El Cid, legendary Spanish hero, who died just before a battle and was strapped to his horse to lead a successful charge against the Moors.

Psychic phenomena, especially anything dealing with "haunted houses," is taken quite seriously in England, and ghosts, under various guises, are more or less taken for granted in Scotland, Ireland and Wales. Guided tours through the great English estates—one way of raising tax money since World War II—usually play up the family ghosts as part of the attraction. One London newspaper a year or so ago featured a long series of daily "authenticated" first-hand ghost stories submitted by readers. This popular series was run under the by-line of Denis Conan Doyle, son of the creator of Sherlock Holmes, and was interrupted only by his death.

In 1934, a group of prominent Britishers interested in things supernatural—Sir Oliver Lodge, an eminent scientist, among them—inaugurated a series of broadcasts over BBC titled "Inquiry into the Unknown." Sir Ernest Bennett, Fellow of Hertford College, Oxford, initiated the broadcasts with a scholarly address over the air on the subject of "Apparitions and Haunted Houses," and appealed to his listeners to forward to him their personal experiences, documented as far as possible, in "the interest of science."

This experiment could hardly be brushed off as silly, considering the names involved. A Lord Chief Justice of England, many titled folk, as well as clergymen, businessmen and professional people were among the 1,300 who responded. Spooks de luxe, indeed!

Out of the mass of reports, Sir Ernest selected fifty "collective cases," so-called because they included the testimony of two or more persons. Only in rare instances was the testimony of only one individual accepted, one exception being Lord Brougham, Chief Justice of England.

The fifty cases, along with half a hundred others gathered by the British Society for Psychological Research, were assembled and published in a book titled *Apparitions and Haunted Houses: A Survey of Evidence,* for which a preface was written by no less a personage than the Dean of St. Paul's Cathedral!

Cambridge University was the first English-speaking educational institution to found a chair for psychical research. And Lord Balfour was president of the British Psychical Research Society at the same time he was Prime Minister of England. After the death of Mackenzie King, Prime Minister of Canada, it was revealed that he, too, had had an ardent interest in spiritualism.

During World War II, one of the New Deal's most prominent financial figures was in the habit of sending to New York for a night club fortuneteller, who would sit in on important meetings and give "advice." The details of these sessions would have made extremely spectacular reading at the time.

We in the United States are more skeptical than the British—or possibly more afraid of being ridiculed if we evince too much interest in such things. But in recent times our savants and scientists have been giving considerable attention to a phase of psychic phenomena that has come to be labeled parapsychology, or *extra-sensory perception,* usually abbreviated "E.S.P."

Meetings have been held on both sides of the Atlantic solemnly to discuss findings along these lines. Invariably, there is mention of the experiments that have been going on for some years at Duke University, at Durham, North Carolina. Professor J. B. Rhine, after conducting a vast number of experiments in telepathy, concluded that certain individuals do unquestionably have E.S.P.

These tests, for the most part, involved such feats as reading off numbers or symbols from cards that were sealed in tin containers, or were otherwise inaccessible to the subject. What useful purpose these experiments achieved isn't immediately evident, since mental telepathy is so commonplace that almost everyone has experienced it. So-called mind reading is practiced so successfully by entertainers who perform in theaters and clubs that one might be tempted to believe they were practicing some sort of black magic. The professional "magician" and professional mindreaders usually insist that it is all done with tricks. However, one couple who do a "mentalist" act in the night clubs—Eddie and Lucille Roberts—privately confessed to me that Lucille, working center stage blindfolded while her husband went about the audience asking questions, frequently "gets" the answers before Eddie has asked the questions. Eddie feels that such close association, over a period of twenty-five years, might easily develop a sixth sense.

Dr. Stanley Jaks, one of the most amazing professional magicians it has been my good luck to know, admitted to me that telepathy does play a large part in some of his tricks, but that he always denies it for publication. Most of the charlatans, he said, are people who do have a modicum of psychic ability, but are forced to resort to trickery when their talent runs out.

One plausible theory on thought transference came from a Western Electric engineer several years ago. After conducting some experiments of his own, he reached the conclusion that the human cranium itself contains the greatest sending and receiving apparatus in the world, one that is capable of transmitting or registering images or messages quite as accurately as a radio or television set, if it could be brought under our conscious control.

More recently, a Harvard scientist attending a convention of the American Association for the Advancement of Sci-

14

ence, Dr. Mary A. Brazier of Harvard Medical School and Massachusetts General Hospital, presented results on brain studies of a number of persons which she claimed established the existence of *two* sensory nerve routes leading to the human brain. It is this "nerve telegraph system," Dr. Brazier maintained, that explains extra-sensory perception.

Neither of these theories, however, could explain the eccentric activities of the human mind which apparently, on occasions, not only contacts the past but is able to reach into the uncharted future. The machine hasn't yet been invented that can trap a ghost, record a mental message or accurately forecast the future. The sand diviners, tea-leaf readers or adepts with the crystal ball—and most certainly the astrologers—would seem to be still ahead of the scientific experimenters in this respect. In nine cases out of ten, the host to unexplainable and frequently pointless "visitations" is taken completely unaware, while engaged in some such mundane occupation as cleaning house or computing his income tax.

Apparently ghosts don't work on schedule. Nor, for that matter, does the human mind; and who is to define *the boundaries of the mind?* Perhaps when we "see" or "hear" ghosts it is because we ourselves, riding that mental magic carpet, have ventured back into the past, like the young man in *Berkeley Square.* In other words, it could be ourselves, thus projected back into the past, who are visiting the ghosts, rather than the ghosts who are visiting us. But this is a subject for endless speculation.

It is quite likely also that many of the daily experiences we have might be regarded as supernatural if we knew more about this fascinating subject. The businessman who acts on inexplicable "hunches"; the dice thrower who calls his shots before the "bones" have hit the floor; the newspaper editor or columnist who, out of twenty hot stories to choose from, invariably picks the one that will make tomorrow's sensational headlines—they may be using their psychic faculties no less than the soothsayer who purports to tell your future.

However, as before stated, this book doesn't set out to prove anything. Of only one thing we can be sure: while perhaps everybody doesn't *believe* a ghost story, practically everybody *loves* a ghost story. So here, for your entertainment, are a few that have entertained me; just a few among the many, many others I've heard but am not permitted to tell.

Danton Walker

New York,
June, 1956

HERE ARE THE STORIES

CARLETON ALSOP'S STORY

This, then, is the story of the haunted penthouse—an anachronism to begin with, since ghosts rightly belong in sad, damp old mansions with creaky floors and rat-infested attics.

You wouldn't expect to find them in a sunlit skyscraper of steel and concrete, would you? Nor would you expect to hear a ghost story as I did, over a frozen daiquiri, to the incongruous accompaniment of rattling maracas and the beat of the bongo drums in what was then New York's latest and smartest Cuban night club—now, alas, gone with the wind.

Nor, for that matter, would you expect terrifying and unearthly experiences to occur to such a *bon vivant* and pillar of café society as my friend Carleton Alsop, concerning ghosts who themselves had been members of café society of a sort only a scant decade before!

To properly understand the background of the story, we have to go back a bit, to the post-World War I period when New York was bursting out of its physical shell—a phenomenon that occurs on an average of once every ten years—and architects of the newer, de luxe apartment houses were adding to them a novelty calculated to attract well-heeled prospective tenants, the *penthouse.*

The new Medical Arts Building on West 57th Street, built specifically to house doctors' suites and a hospital, had such a penthouse, but it was not for rent. A woman who had just fallen heir to a twelve-million-dollar fortune fell in love with the penthouse—or, rather, her paramour did—and offered to rent it, but was refused. Whereupon she bought the entire building, paying $1,300,000 cash for it.

The woman was Edna Crawford Champion and the man to whom she gave the building as a present was her lover, Charles Brazelle. Edna's husband, Albert Champion, was dead—from an alleged heart attack following a brutal beat-

19

ing administered by Brazelle in the bar of the Hotel Crillon in Paris just a year before.

How this tragic triumvirate happened to get together is a story in itself, and one that makes you believe in destiny. Albert Champion had come to the United States from France to engage in professional bicycle racing, then in vogue. When racing engagements became scarce he drifted to Detroit and became affiliated with the automotive business, which he was destined shortly to revolutionize. Champion invented and patented a little gadget called the spark plug, and almost before he could realize what was happening had become a millionaire several times over.

Both Champion and the little French wife who came to join him in Detroit were typical middle-class people, totally unaccustomed to luxurious living. Mrs. Champion found it hard to adjust herself to this suddenly acquired wealth. So, eventually, while on a business trip to New York, Mr. Champion found another woman who was both eager and willing to help spend his money. This was Edna Crawford, a luscious blonde beauty, daughter of a St. Louis seamstress, who had come to New York looking for just such a catch.

It was love—or infatuation—at first sight, on Champion's part. But Edna, like many another *femme fatale* in similar circumstances, held out for matrimony. So, after considerable negotiation, Champion persuaded his French wife to divorce him, settling on her a cool million in return. He then married Edna and took her to live in Detroit. But Edna didn't like Detroit and apparently the dislike was mutual, since she shortly persuaded her husband to move to New York.

Champion, in common with many other elderly husbands who have just married young wives, was insanely jealous of his bride where the possibility of other men's attentions was concerned. He had a quirk peculiar to many rich men: he would shower clothes, furs and jewelry on his wife but refused to give her a bank account of her own, or even any sizable amounts of cash, apparently fearful that she might become independent of him.

A sudden business trip to Paris necessitated Champion's taking off alone, with arrangements for Edna to follow. On the day she was to arrive in Paris, Champion found himself too involved in some business transaction to meet her at the railroad station, so persuaded an old friend, whom he could trust, to chaperon her to their hotel. The friend was Barney Oldfield, the former automobile racer. Champion evidently failed to convey to Oldfield his fears about Edna's susceptibility to the attractions of younger, handsomer men, for on the way to the station Oldfield bumped into another friend and invited him to come along.

The friend was Charles Brazelle—debonair, handsome and years younger than Champion. Both Edna and Charlie maintained afterward that it was a case of love at first sight —or, again, infatuation; on her part, at least.

Brazelle came of a good background: his father was a French mining engineer, a graduate of the Sorbonne, and his mother the daughter of an American shipbuilder. But he was a fortune-hunter who had a way with women and it took him no time at all to decide that Edna Champion was easy prey.

One secret meeting quickly followed another before Champion discovered what was going on. He was furious, threatened to cut off Edna without a cent and refused to give her even ordinary spending money.

Instead of obeying her husband's wishes, Edna stubbornly continued to see Brazelle and it was while she was enjoying a rendezvous with him at the Crillon Bar that Champion came on them together. There was a violent scene and Brazelle struck Champion. The older man staggered away and a few hours later was discovered dead in his hotel room. Brazelle's alibi to the Paris police was that Champion "had a weak heart."

After a superficial investigation, doubtless speeded up with financial "persuasion," the police dropped the investigation and Champion's demise was written off as death from natural causes.

As Champion's widow, Edna suddenly found herself possessed of money beyond her wildest dreams, a fortune of around twelve million dollars. Marriage with Charles Brazelle however was out of the question, for the time being at least, since he already had a wife somewhere. Edna would have to be content for the time with having him as her paramour.

They returned together to New York and were soon engaged in the delightful pastime of squandering the old man's wealth. One of Charlie's whims was to live in a newfangled apartment with a penthouse, so Edna set out to find one for him. It was because of this urgency that she purchased the building at 57 West 57th Street.

Decorators were brought in and the penthouse apartment, which included two other floors, was done over to the queen's taste, and quite regardless of expense. Special floors were laid; false walls and ceilings installed; stained glass windows, marble mantels and rare tapestries imported from Europe. For the playroom, Edna ordered a forty-foot mural painted. The scene was a Venetian carnival, the central figures of which were Charlie and Edna—with Edna, astonishingly, quite nude but for mask and domino and a pair of high-heeled shoes.

A secret stairway was built to connect Charlie's apartments on the lower floor to Edna's quarters above. Outside, on the terraces, exotic plants began to bloom. Inside, fountains bubbled under artificial moonlight; monkeys and peacocks in gaudy colors capered over gold and silver walls. On the top floor, in the penthouse proper, a special room was built to house a magnificent carved bed, over which hung a canopy of pure gold cloth—the ecclesiastical vestments filched from a Russian church—cost, thirty thousand dollars.

It took five years to decorate the place and it wasn't completed even when Edna lay dying, a pitiful victim of drugs and drink and a blow inflicted by a telephone thrown at her by her lover in one of their numerous drunken quarrels.

For a long time, Charlie had kept Edna virtually a prisoner in the apartment, watched over by spying French servants. After the telephone incident, Edna's indignant relatives managed to get to her and Charlie was ejected, bag and baggage. Bodyguards were installed to keep Brazelle away. He tried to return many times, hiding for days in the doctors' suites throughout the building, to which he had duplicate keys.

Charlie made one last attempt to get to Edna the night she died. He was intercepted by her bodyguards, horribly beaten and thrown bodily from her bedroom window to the terrace below. Charlie died soon afterward, indirectly from his injuries, and his corpse lay in the morgue for ten days before being identified by a long-lost brother.

Brazelle, to give him credit, had managed his affairs well.

22

He had collected the rentals from the hospital building, installed a brokerage office on the second floor to handle his accounts and, for a short time, operated a night club in the basement, the *Boeuf sur le Toit*, copied and named after a *boîte* in Paris.

But neither Charlie's banker nor his broker could account for the large sums of cash that had passed through his hands. The supposition was that he had hidden away much of the money somewhere in the apartment, possibly behind the many secret panels that lined the walls or upstairs in the engine room on the roof where, for some mysterious reason, he spent a good deal of his time. After Edna's death, her relatives organized several treasure hunts, but without success. Charlie carried his financial secrets, at least, to his grave.

And now the stage is set for our modern ghost story!

The penthouse remained unoccupied, its furnishings intact, for quite a time. Carleton Alsop, then an executive of a sound recording company, inspected it and, knowing nothing of its grim background, decided it was just the place for an urban honeymoon with his bride, the former Princess Melikov de Somethie, wealthy American widow of a Russian nobleman and a relative of Mrs. John D. Rockefeller, Jr.

What appealed to both of them, principally, was the terrace that would serve as a good dog run for the four magnificent great Danes that Alsop owned.

The Alsops' happiness in their newfound eyrie was brief. Quarrels, unreasonable and violent, broke out over matters which, Alsop himself would tell you, could not be traced to the normal human difficulties of the newlywed. Cocktail parties—too many of them—especially had unexpected and disastrous results.

It was not long before the atmosphere of the place began to affect Mrs. Alsop so strangely that her husband became alarmed. She would sit for hours before a mirror, bemoaning the fact that she would soon lose her youth and beauty. Though she was born to a family of great wealth and had inherited a fortune, she would worry and fret about money, insisting on petty economies and always eating breakfast in the butler's pantry in preference to the elaborate breakfast room. She would send notes to her husband in mid-afternoon, complaining that she shouldn't be left alone, although the house was full of servants at the time. She was once found wandering around on the fifteenth floor of the building, in a half-hysterical condition.

This behavior might not have seemed of any special significance if Alsop hadn't discovered that Mrs. Champion had behaved in the *selfsame manner*. A psychiatrist was called in and it was on his advice that they decided to make certain changes in their mode of living.

The Alsops moved to the two top floors, gave up the lower floor and sealed the secret stairway that Charlie Brazelle had used. Alsop ripped out the fantastic trimmings of the Russian boudoir and transformed it into a smart modern bedroom. But no amount of paint and alterations seemed to change the atmosphere. It was the behavior of the dogs, the four great Danes, that was the hardest thing to account for.

At night the dogs were kept upstairs in the penthouse bedroom. The two newlyweds would frequently be awakened by their whining. Turning on the lights, they would find the animals standing four abreast, with taut muscles and hackles on end, gazing through the bedroom's glass doors—*at nothing.*

Two of the dogs, with all the indications of a nervous breakdown, were returned to the kennels, leaving behind one adult and a puppy. The puppy became the greatest offender of all, frequently hiding under the bed and refusing to come out.

Skeptics may prefer the theory that dogs always behave strangely in the presence of death, and death was taking its toll regularly in the hospital below. But this could not explain other things that disturbed the animals and the Alsops themselves, such as noises that resembled the nervous click of French heels on the tiled floor below, and the sound of strange, unintelligible quarrels that floated up the stairs.

In less than a year, Alsop's wife had left him; simply walked out of the place, vowing never to return. He remained on, alone but for the housekeeper who had worked for the Champions and still continued to care for Champion's dog, a sad-eyed, aged chow that would stand for hours on end in the center of a room, whimpering mournfully for no reason at all.

After his wife left him, Alsop attempted to cheer himself with convivial friends and drinking parties. At one of these, a guest went upstairs to visit the bathroom and returned, white and shaking, unable to explain what had come over him. On another occasion, a woman guest—an Englishwoman with a high-sounding title—vowed that someone had followed her down the stairs. When all present denied any complicity, she indignantly stated that she "disliked practical jokes!"

Now any dog-fancier can tell you that a great Dane is one of the friendliest as well as the most courageous of animals. It wasn't a pretty sight to see one of these noble beasts convulsed with fear, its tail between its legs, groveling at the feet of its master. Yet this is what happened when Alsop, either alone or in company of friends, attempted to investigate the mysterious footsteps on the floor below. The dogs simply refused to accompany him; nothing could induce them to go below.

What finally brought Alsop himself to the verge of a nervous collapse, however, was the fact that when he had reached the floor below, either alone or with friends, the sounds ceased, *only to be repeated immediately on the floor overhead.*

Eventually, Alsop wound up in the hospital—the hospital beneath the haunted penthouse. When his nerves had recovered sufficiently, he determined to sublet the place, at no matter what financial loss, and seek less troubled quarters.

Several years after these happenings, I visited the penthouse in Alsop's company. He was pleased to find that the atmosphere had changed enormously. The lower floor, where Charlie Brazelle had made his home, was occupied by a famous plastic surgeon. The two-story penthouse proper had been rented by a doctor from Vermont. Currier & Ives prints graced the walls where monkeys and peacocks had once capered over gold-leaf wallpaper, and the playroom rang to the happy laughter of a child. The spell, it seemed, was broken.

Off in a storeroom, put there because no one knew what else to do with such a white elephant, lingered the forty-foot mural of a Venetian carnival in which Charlie and Edna posed as central figures—Edna nude but for mask, domino and the *high-heeled shoes*. I wonder what ever became of it?

DOROTHY MASSEY'S STORY

Animals figure frequently in stories of haunted houses or bewitched persons, more especially dogs and cats. It is traditional that a rat will desert a ship that is headed for disaster, but I never knew that a mouse also gets the message until Mrs. Raymond Massey told me of her experiences, which might be labeled "The Masseys' Migrating Mice."

The exact street addresses and correct names of the people involved can't be given, unfortunately, due to certain laws of libel which are intended to protect property values or the reputations of individuals. However, I personally knew several of the people involved, and New York newspaper morgues contain clippings of the incidents mentioned in this story.

Back in the 1940's the Raymond Masseys, weary of camping out in hotels in New York or California, where Ray's movie commitments frequently took him, decided to purchase a town house in New York as a *pied-à-terre* that they eventually could call home. After the usual search, they hit on a block in the East 80's which contained a number of charming old brownstone mansions, by now something of a drug on the market because of their size and the prevalent servant problem.

The house they eventually acquired wasn't the first one that struck Mrs. Massey's fancy. The one they first looked at, across the street, was in her opinion more attractive and a better buy. But Ray didn't like it and said he felt he wouldn't feel comfortable there.

"At that time," Dorothy explains, "no one could have felt comfortable in any of them. It was February and all the houses were cold, with that penetrating cold one meets in long-vacant dwellings. But that one house—the one Ray didn't like—had a chill that was not of this earth. He said it felt to him more like a tomb."

27

Dorothy, being accustomed to actors' hunches and respecting them, didn't insist. The house they did settle on was, after a complete restoration job, completely charming, and Mrs. Massey was reconciled to the choice. She thought no more about the house across the way until a series of curious and inexplicable incidents again brought it to her attention.

While out walking her dog one morning she encountered a lady who was also giving her pooch an airing. As usually happens when dog-fanciers meet, they struck up a conversation and Dorothy learned that the stranger was her neighbor, living across the street, in the house that Ray hadn't liked.

"We looked at your house before we bought ours," Mrs. Massey remarked. "I thought it more attractive than the one we did buy, but my husband didn't like it, for some reason or other, and I didn't argue with him."

"It *is* an attractive house," the lady answered. "But there's one thing about it that bothers me: we have mice. We have tried practically everything to get rid of them but they just refuse to get out. They seem to be even more attached to the place than we are!"

It was some time after this casual meeting that Mrs. Massey, glancing out of the front window of their second-story library, noticed a peculiar movement going on across the way. From the English basement of the house that Ray hadn't liked there was a sudden exodus of mice.

"They came out in groups, in a panicky sort of way, confused and scurrying along the gutter. Then one or two got brave and made the bold dash across the street to my house. I immediately ran to the phone to call the exterminator.

"I didn't see if or how they got in," Dorothy went on, "but get in they certainly did. All of a sudden, we had *plenty* of mice. We tried poison and traps and just about everything else you can think of, but got no results until the plumber brought around a couple of cats. They're still the best mousetraps—but that's not the point of the story.

"A few days after the mice started coming in, Ray called my attention to a front-page story in one of the morning papers. A Mrs. B., described as socially prominent and well-to-do, had committed suicide.

" 'Why,' I exclaimed, 'that must be the woman who lives

28

across the street! Check the address.' Ray did and, sure enough, it was the house across the way—the house from which the mice had moved out the week before.

"After the woman's death, the rest of her family moved away and the place was put on the market. I don't remember just when it was taken over again but it was pretty apparent *why* it was taken over. The new occupant was a gorgeous blonde, a former 'Follies' beauty, who was being installed by a wealthy playboy, the nationally known executive of a big oil company; you, of course, recognize his name. He was always getting married or divorced or something, and his extra-marital affairs invariably got mentioned in the gossip columns.

"When he died—of natural causes, I hope—there was a big battle over his estate. As might be expected, his first wife got most of the money and his gal friends had to be content with the furs and jewels and other finery that he had given them while he was still alive. The blonde living across the way was dispossessed, literally put out on the sidewalk, gilded DuBarry bed and all. But again, that is not the point of this story.

"Just before his death made front-page news, those darned mice moved out *again*. I happened to be standing at the front window, minding my own business—adjusting a Venetian blind, as I remember—when I saw it happen. And again I had to go through the routine of seeing that the mice didn't take up permanent residence in *my* house.

"This mouse hegira was beginning to get on my nerves and I found myself watching the house across the way for further manifestations, almost as a morning ritual. However, nothing happened again for a long time.

"After remaining vacant a while, the house found another purchaser. Neither Ray nor I knew anything about our new neighbor, but we heard through the local grapevine that he was a solid, successful businessman and we thought no more about it. And then, one day, it happened again—the mouse migration, I mean. I was watering some plants in the window-box when I saw the little creatures going through the same rigamarole, and I went cold all over. What was going to happen *now*?

"I kept nervously anticipating some sort of bad news from across the way, and I didn't have to wait long to get it. While Ray and I were having breakfast, he called my attention to an item on the front page of the *New York Times*. A prominent businessman who flew his own private plane and was returning, as I recall it, from some trip to Canada, had cracked up over the Hudson and drowned before rescuers could reach him. Neither of us knew the man but we both instantly recognized his home address—*the house across the way!*

"And then the most extraordinary thing happened. The mice that were in my basement—we hadn't got rid of them all, in spite of traps, cats and every other precaution—now started moving out! I kept a careful watch on them and discovered that they were leaving my basement and going back across the street, where they had originally come from!"

Mrs. Massey, who has a delightful sense of humor—especially for one trained in the legal profession, as she was—laughed.

"No, nothing particularly sinister happened to us after the mice moved out, except that our furnace blew up! Nobody was hurt and we were fully protected by insurance, so I suppose there is no angle to the story there.

"Sometime after that, Ray and I fell in love with a place in Connecticut that had belonged to the Larry Tibbetts and decided to move there and sell our town house in the 80's.

"In connection with transferring the property, I took occasion to delve into the history of some of the houses in our block. I then learned that the house across the way, which seemed to be connected with bad luck of one kind or another, had been built by a distinguished lawyer, a partner in one of the most prominent legal firms in the country. He apparently didn't live there very long and it was after he had left the place that he attempted suicide. He had gone into Presbyterian Hospital for some physical check-ups and, for reasons never explained, escaped from the attendants and run down to the Hudson, where he tried to drown himself. They fished him out of the river in fair shape, and he continued to live a long time after that—but he never explained why he had made the try.

"I don't know what the house across the way had to do with it, if anything," Mrs. Massey concluded, "but looking back, it is a bit disturbing, isn't it?"

DONALD ROCKWELL'S STORY

Another story concerning the strange behavior of animals in a time of crisis was told me by Donald S. Rockwell, manager of Columbia Pictures of Panama, Inc., who now resides in the Republic of Panama, but was in New York on a business trip when I met him.

The story devolves from a personal tragedy in his family which is still very vivid in his mind—the suicide of his younger sister, Ruth Rockwell. The incident made front-page news at the time, not only in the United States but also abroad, and continued to be written about in magazines long afterward because of its peculiar circumstances. Her death marked the first time in history that a woman had committed suicide by leaping from a plane.

"At the time, I was manager of the Sound-on-Disc Division of the Columbia Phonograph Company, with offices on Fifth Avenue," Mr. Rockwell told me. "My wife and I were living at Brook Farm, Crestwood, in Westchester County, and I commuted daily to my office via the New York Central. Our near neighbors at the time, I recall, were the retired actress, Laura Nelson Hall, and William Robison, the songwriter and radio broadcaster.

"For several months my sister Ruth had been visiting us, occupying a guest room on the second floor of our house. She was eighteen, a recent graduate of a seminary near Brewster, New York, and had everything in life to look forward to. However, she was moody and apparently obsessed with the idea of death. She was very fond of Sidney Lanier's poems, especially one touching on 'the beauty of death,' and after she had left us we found in her room a book on astrology, with certain marked passages dealing with the end of life.

"My mother was a deep student of astrology and the so-called occult mystery teachings, hence a firm believer in reincarnation. From earliest childhood Ruth had absorbed much from lectures on these subjects and discussions of kindred topics.

"On Armistice Day, November 11, 1930, I had gone to my office as usual, intending to put in only half a day, but found myself detained there by a business emergency. Around three o'clock I received a phone call from the police at Tuckahoe, asking me to remain at the office until they could reach there with my wife, saying they would explain later.

"Around four o'clock my wife arrived at the office in the company of two policemen from Tuckahoe, who had driven her down in a police car. She then broke the sad news that my sister Ruth had leaped from a plane over Valley Stream, Long Island, and was killed. The plane was one of those small ones, holding no more than one or two passengers, which in those days took sightseers up for a brief ride, charging something like five dollars per passenger. The Valley Stream police identified Ruth by papers in her purse and phoned the Tuckahoe police, who then notified my wife.

"The pilot remembered that she had seemed very nervous when she boarded the plane. Later, he turned around to see how she was faring and noticed that her hands were clasped, in an attitude of prayer. A moment later, he felt the plane lurch, whereupon he looked around again and found her gone.

"When my wife and I reached home, after dining in the city, we discovered that the furnace fire had gone out and the house was quite cold. We went upstairs, but instead of going to bed immediately, we sat down to try to reconstruct the events of the day. Still wearing her coat, my wife had seated herself on the bed, propped up with the pillows at her back, and pulled a comforter over her knees for warmth.

"She recalled that when Ruth left the house that morning she had remarked that she 'might not be back in the afternoon.' My wife then recounted to me the strange behavior of the dog.

"The animal, a great Dane named Rajah of Rangoon, was an extremely intelligent dog, gentle and well-behaved at all times. Both my wife and I were very fond of him, and Ruth shared this feeling. I remember seeing her, many times, seated in a high-backed Italian chair in the living room with

Rajah sitting on the floor beside her, putting up his head to be stroked, turning it first to one side, then the other.

"My wife recalled that about three o'clock that afternoon she was seated in the living room, when the dog suddenly ran upstairs but immediately returned, carrying a pillow in his mouth, which he put down at her feet. He then raced again to the second floor, returning this time with a coat, which my wife recognized as one of Ruth's. A third time, Rajah went upstairs and came back with one of Ruth's hats. He then lay down on the floor, with his head on these objects and emitted great convulsive sobs, like a human being.

"Quite baffled by this performance, my wife took the coat and hat upstairs to Ruth's room and put the pillow back where it belonged, on the day bed on which she slept.

"About a half-hour later came the phone call from the Tuckahoe police, notifying her of Ruth's death. Apparently the strange behavior of the dog had taken place *almost exactly coincident with Ruth's leap from the plane.*

"Rajah was still distraught when we returned home that night. He was lying on a scatter rug in the bedroom when my wife seated herself on the bed. A few minutes later he leaped up and, barking furiously, bounded across the room to the casement windows that looked out on the driveway. Then he turned to the bedside and put his paws on my wife's knees, as if to protect her, meanwhile snarling and growling in a way we had never known him to do.

"A moment later, he returned to the window, where he resumed his savage snarling, with his forefeet on the window sill and the hackles standing up on his neck—something we had also never seen before. I hurried to the window and looked out. There was no one in the yard or on the driveway, and the brilliantly lighted street was deserted. Rajah was evidently disturbed by something that we couldn't see. After a time, we managed to quiet him down.

"Glancing at my watch, I noted that this episode occurred around 9:00 P.M. In a farewell note Ruth had written, '*If there is a spirit world, I will attempt to communicate with someone in the family at nine o'clock at night.*'

"Several times after that the dog behaved strangely. Once he dashed out of the house and approached a bush in the yard, barking in an enraged manner. Investigation revealed nothing near the bush to account for his fury. On several occasions, he seized my wife's dress in his teeth and attempted to detour her around something—*something invisible to her*—in the dining room and hall. At one time, my wife said she felt she had seen a stranger, a dark-skinned man resembling a Hindu, pass through the house. I began to fear that the shock of Ruth's death and the strange behavior of the dog were beginning to undermine her health, for she had become intensely nervous.

"After a few weeks, however, these manifestations ceased and things returned to normal in our home. Rajah never again acted so strangely, but I did notice him many times sitting beside Ruth's favorite chair—the high-backed Italian chair—and putting up his head, apparently to be stroked by someone who wasn't there."

GUTHRIE MC CLINTIC'S STORY

Theatrical people would seem to be particularly susceptible to "hauntings," possibly because they themselves exist in a world peopled by imaginary beings. Among the great people of the theater of recent memory who were fascinated by the psychic or supernatural, the names of David Belasco, Charles Frohman, William Gillette and Tyrone Power (father of the present-day star) come readily to mind.

London's Drury Lane Theatre is haunted by a ghost and one that has been seen—according to theatrical writer J. Wentworth Day—by charwomen, firemen, actors and even some members of the audiences at that famous playhouse. Judging by its clothes, it seems to be the ghost of an eighteenth century dandy, who must have been murdered sometime around 1780 and his body bricked up in a small anteroom of the theater. Workmen, opening up a wall several years ago, came across the skeleton, still clad in the shreds of a smart gray riding habit, and with a dagger still sticking through his ribs. The surmise is that he had been flirting with one of the Drury Lane actresses and got his come-uppance from a jealous rival.

Maqueen Pope, who wrote a history of the Drury Lane which he presented to the British Museum, claims that this is the only authentic ghost that he knows, and adds that its visitations are looked upon as a good omen because it only shows up just before the theater has a hit! Could any publicity man, Mr. Wentworth Day inquires, ask for a better ghost than that?

There was another sort of ghost, or at least another type of visitation, that brought glad tidings, and one much closer to our time. This was the long-time "familiar" of Guthrie McClintic, to whom he admittedly owes most of his success, but more particularly the success, financial and otherwise, of *The Barretts of Wimpole Street*.

35

I dug the story out of McClintic while interviewing him in connection with the World War II tour of *The Barretts* which scored an unexpected success with our troops overseas. I asked him if he considered the play his greatest theatrical hit.

"Not only my greatest theatrical hit, but one of the greatest hits in theatrical history," he answered. "It ran for more than a year at the Empire Theatre and after that we took it on a seventeen-thousand-mile tour of the country. There have been two successful revivals on Broadway and since its first presentation the play has grossed more than two million dollars. During the war, we played it for six months overseas for GI audiences in Italy, France and Holland. The tour was scheduled for eight weeks but it stretched out to six months 'by popular demand.'

"The most unusual thing about *The Barretts*, however," McClintic went on, "is how close it came to never being produced at all." Then, cogitating a moment, as if questioning himself on the wisdom of confiding such an odd story to a newspaper columnist, McClintic added: "It was an anonymous telephone call from a lady—I presume you might call her a fortuneteller—that turned the trick."

"Tell me more," I urged.

"When the play first came into our hands, it had already been turned down by no fewer than twenty-eight producers on Broadway, though we didn't know this at the time. Gilbert Miller, who had Kit—meaning my wife, Katharine Cornell—under contract then, didn't like the play and said so, emphatically. So, after much discussion, they came to a parting of the ways. Kit then bought the play for me to produce, though not as a vehicle for herself. It was I who persuaded her that she should play Elizabeth Barrett. I had conceived the idea that it would be an effective novelty for Kit to launch it under her own producing banner with herself as star—'Katharine Cornell presents Miss Cornell in *The Barretts of Wimpole Street*, directed by Guthrie McClintic.' The idea took with all of us and we enthusiastically started rehearsals.

"The play seemed jinxed from the start. After a week of rehearsals, Kit reverted to her original notion that the role

36

was not for her. This was unusual because when Miss Cornell makes up her mind about anything she seldom changes it.

"About this time I came down with flu and was out about nine days. Kit carried on with the rehearsals in my absence, but when I recovered I found she was still unconvinced. If she declined to play the role, my idea of her becoming an actress-manager would be discarded and the whole scheme would fall through. And I also felt that if Kit didn't play the leading role, *The Barretts* would be a flop. I found myself also beginning to lose faith in the play.

"Things were looking pretty dark and I was on the verge of giving up the whole project when the matter was climaxed by a telephone call. We were still in conference when the phone rang.

"Stanley Gilkey, then my secretary, answered it and came back into the room to say that 'a friend' wished to speak to me on important business. I lost my temper, told Gilkey that I was in no mood to talk to idiots who announced themselves as 'a friend.' Then, suddenly, acting on a hunch, I changed my mind and said I would take the call.

" 'McClintic speaking,' I said into the receiver. Then, with no preamble of identification, a woman's voice answered.

" 'Nothing to worry about,' the anonymous voice said over the phone. 'You are about to have your greatest success to date,' and before I had a chance to reply the party hung up."

I laughed, a little incredulously.

"And you went ahead and produced *The Barretts* on the strength of that?" I asked.

McClintic's face broke into a smile.

"Well, it *does* take a bit of explaining," he said, rather apologetically. "But, you see, I had good reason to listen to anonymous tips from mysterious sources. It was on a similar tip—and incidentally from the same party—that I attained my first success in the theater. In fact, I might say, my *entire* success in the theater dates from such a tip."

"Then you knew the source of the anonymous telephone call?"

"Yes," McClintic answered slowly, "but it's quite a long story. . . ."

And here it is, in Guthrie McClintic's own words:

37

"It was around 1909, I think, that I was first bitten by the theatrical bug. I was living with my parents in Seattle, where I was born. About the only theatrical fare we had was dished up by some obscure stock companies and an occasional visiting troupe from Broadway. When I say 'obscure,' I am not disparaging them. Some of the best actors in our theater were groomed in just such companies. One we had in Seattle was operated by a man named Taylor, whose leading lady was his young and pretty wife, Laurette Taylor.

"But to get on with the story.

"My first theater job was with the Bowman Repertory Company, in which I impersonated a cornet player in a stage band that didn't play a note. When the troupe moved to another town, I went along, and we got as far as Walla Walla when I was yanked home by an irate father. Neither of my parents cared for the theater, but my father was just about as Victorian in his prejudices as was Edward Moulton-Barrett.

"By this time, my mind was made up and he knew it. So, rather than see his young hopeful grow up into a third-rate ham, he decided to make the best of it and see that I got what, to his mind, was a proper start. So he staked me to a trip to New York and a course at the Academy of Dramatic Art, where I was to remain long enough either to make a success or get it out of my system.

"My cash allowance in New York was just about enough, as Alexander Woollcott once put it, to keep body and soul apart. But I located a furnished room up around Morningside Heights at a price I could afford—$3.50 per week. My landlady was a woman from Texas, a Mrs. Heinsohn—truly a Southern gentlewoman she was—who had two small sons and an old maid relative, "Cousin Lulu," living with her and was eking out a meager income by renting out a couple of rooms in her flat.

"I finished my course at the Academy and then began that long, lean apprenticeship that most young actors have to go through as part of their preparation for the most fascinating but unpredictable profession on earth.

"Every day I made the rounds of the casting offices, always getting the same answer—'No!' Sometimes the agents, or their front-office girls, didn't even bother to speak, just shook their heads when they saw me come in.

"In the entire year after I left the Academy, I had worked exactly five weeks and one day, in a couple of out-of-town productions, and things were getting pretty desperate financially. There had been an occasional handout from home, but by this time I would have starved rather than call on my father for aid and give him the satisfaction of saying 'I told you so.'

"One day I was sitting on a bench in Bryant Park, feeling particularly low, when a boy I had known at the Academy greeted me and enthusiastically, and a little patronizingly, informed me that he had just been signed by the great producer, Winthrop Ames, for a role in *Prunella*. He then inquired, actor-fashion, about my own activities. I replied, actor-fashion, that I was mulling over a couple of offers. (I don't know what it is, but out-of-work actors always pretend they are considering *two* offers simultaneously, never just one.) Anyway, when he departed, practically treading on air, I lost no time getting over to the Ames office to try my luck.

"Mr. Ames was not seeing people, I was informed, but his director, Mr. George Foster Platt, would grant me an interview. Platt was an austere, rather forbidding personality, who struck terror in the hearts of fledgling actors. At any rate, he affected me that way when I found myself seated in his presence.

"After Platt had informed me, quite politely, that there was nothing in prospect for me, I continued to sit, fairly frozen to my chair. Finally, to terminate the interview, he thrust his hand across the table and said firmly, 'Good afternoon, Mr. McClintic.'

"I was so flustered at the thought of shaking hands with him that in my awkwardness and confusion I knocked over the fancy inkwell that stood on his desk. I think that was the most horrible moment of my life, watching that pool of ink spreading over his papers. I tried to do something about it but Platt, by now in a cold rage, told me to go—to *get out* —and called in his assistant.

"I did get out of the office, somehow, in a state of mixed rage and mortification, convinced that my career had ended even before it had begun. At that moment I was feeling reckless enough, almost, to do anything, even to heaving a brick through Mr. Winthrop Ames's window.

"Instead, I walked over to the Astor Hotel, where the stationery was free, and sat down to indite a letter to the great man, telling him precisely what I thought and how I felt. I meant to pull no punches, and I didn't.

"Before becoming a producer in his own right, Winthrop Ames had directed the destinies of the New Theatre (long since gone and forgotten) and Broadway always suspected him of being overly pro-British in his choice of actors and plays. Perhaps to offset this impression, he had posted a ten-thousand-dollar offer for the best American play written by an American playwright, and the gesture made front-page news (this was in 1913, before the world was concerned with more important things).

"I don't recall now exactly what I wrote, but I know that I poured into that letter all the bitter invective of a thwarted and ambitious kid. I accused Mr. Ames of bias against native actors and chided him for offering ten-thousand-dollar prizes for native plays when so much young native *acting* talent was walking the streets, hungry. Nor was I modest in setting forth my own qualifications, nor my ideas on the future of the theater.

"By the time I had finished the letter—and it was a masterpiece of sorts—I had cooled off a bit and decided that caution, at least, might be the better part of valor. I would not send the letter, I said to myself—well, not just yet. So I sealed the envelope, but instead of addressing it and adding a stamp, I merely wrote the date in the upper right-hand corner, where the stamp belongs. I then thrust the letter into my inside pocket and started for home.

"In those days, I frequently walked home to save subway fare, and Morningside Heights, I assure you, is quite a walk from Times Square. When I got to my room that evening, I tossed the letter into my trunk and then forgot all about it. Next day, I was back on Broadway, making the rounds again—but studiedly avoiding the offices of producer Winthrop Ames.

"It was just five weeks after this incident that I came home one evening, hot and tired, and in a new low state of depression, actually bordering on desperation, after having made the usual dreary rounds of the casting offices. I had thrown off my clothes, preparatory to going to bed, and was sitting there mulling the possibilities of getting a job as a

40

messenger, or an elevator operator, or just about anything else, when there was a knock at my door.

"It was my landlady, Mrs. Heinsohn. No, she wasn't coming to dispossess me, or even to demand the back rent.

" 'Mr. McClintic'—she always called me 'Mr. McClintic' —'the table wishes to speak to you.'

At this point I (the author) interrupted the flow of McClintic's story.

"A *table?*" I inquired.

"Yes, a table. I knew immediately what Mrs. Heinsohn meant. Whether for diversion, or because she couldn't afford more expensive amusements, she entertained herself most of the time evenings by sitting in her living room, communicating with the spirit world—or what she firmly believed to be the spirit world—via a code of table-tipping. I remember hearing the table thumping away, many times far into the night, and I knew that Mrs. Heinsohn was getting messages from some 'familiar,' usually a relative long since deceased, who addressed her as 'Cousin Ada.'

"Most people suspect some sort of trickery in such goings-on, but I assure you there was no trickery here. Mrs. Heinsohn always worked alone, and she never exploited her gift, if that's the word for it, professionally. She had discovered this power quite accidentally and was as much astonished by it as anyone else.

"I do not know, of course, what mysterious force gave her the power, but I had seen her raise a table—that is, one side of a table, and a heavy table, while the other two legs remained on the floor—merely by laying a finger on it. And there the table would remain, in a state of suspended animation, so to speak, until she commanded or requested it to come down.

"To obtain answers to questions, she would slowly recite the alphabet aloud. When she had reached a certain letter, the table, leaning back on two legs, would come down with a resounding thump. By this long and laborious process, she would get her 'messages.'

"So, when she knocked on my door that particular night, I knew what she was talking about. I threw on a bathrobe

41

and followed her into the living room, taking along a pencil and paper, at her suggestion, on which to write down the portentous message.

"Mrs. Heinsohn sat quietly, with her hands on the table, until it indicated its desire to 'speak' by suddenly raising two legs off the floor. At her direction, I started slowly to chant the letters of the alphabet aloud. Nothing happened until I reached the letter 'M,' when the table came down with a thud. I then continued with the alphabet, the table, meanwhile, having again risen on its hind legs. From 'N' to 'Z' nothing happened, so I started all over again. On the very first letter, the table gave a thump, so I wrote down the letter 'A.' The process was repeated, and this time the table rapped on the letter 'I' and again on the letter 'L.'

"Well, to make a long story shorter, the letters thus meticulously thumped out by the table were

MAILTHATWHICHYOUHAVEWRITTEN
YOURENTIREFUTUREDEPENDSUPONIT

"Divided into words, this read *'mail that which you have written your entire future depends upon it.'* And that was all.

"When we tried to get further details, such as where the message was supposed to come from, and what it meant, the table refused to budge.

"Neither I nor Mrs. Heinsohn had the slightest idea what the message was about, and she was not only disappointed but a trifle cross when I failed to understand the message.

"Then, suddenly and as sharply as if it were an electric shock, the meaning of those cryptic words came to me. *The letter in my trunk, of course!*

"I hurried to my room, got out the letter, addressed it to Winthrop Ames, Esq., at his Little Theatre address and added a stamp. By then it was well past midnight, but I dressed and set out to find the nearest letter box. I found it, I distinctly remember, at the corner of 115th Street and Riverside Drive, and dropped the letter in. By now, it was 2:30 A.M. of this hot summer morning in June.

"Two days went by with nothing happening. On the third day, I had an answer. It was *signed personally by Winthrop Ames!* He stated that my letter had interested him 'enormously,' and invited me, in the most cordial and gentlemanly fashion, to pay him a visit at his office!

"No words in any vocabulary could do justice to the thrill

that letter gave me. Nor could mere words do justice to the disappointment and chagrin I felt when, on showing up bright and early next day at his office, I was told that Mr. Ames was ill and couldn't see me. And again, the next day, when his secretary apologized and set the appointment two days further ahead.

"The third time I showed up, Mr. Ames' secretary, Helen Ingersoll, told me that he had decided to waive the interview and sign me to a contract, sight unseen, if I were agreeable. *If I were agreeable!* The great man had liked my ideas on the theater, it seemed, and was willing to hire me on the strength of what I had put into my letter.

"The job was to be assistant stage manager, at twenty-five dollars a week, with a new play titled *Her Own Money* —to be directed by that same George Foster Platt upon whose desk I had splattered ink.

"That was the beginning of an association that was to last nine years. Oddly enough, I never saw Winthrop Ames to talk to until some eight months after I started working for him. In February of the following year, he called me in, this time to appoint me full-fledged stage manager for the all-star production of *The Truth*, scheduled for Spring production at the Little Theatre.

"At the conclusion of the run of *The Truth*, Mr. Ames again sent for me, this time to ask how I felt about working for him on a yearly basis, instead of just a play-to-play arrangement. I had finished my apprenticeship, he said, and from then on was to be identified as his *assistant*. Just fourteen months after I had retreated so ignominiously from George Foster Platt's offices, I was occupying his job; sitting in the same office and, in fact, using the same ink-stained desk.

"After nearly a decade of this mutually pleasant association, Mr. Ames called me in one day and asked how I would like to become a producer on my own; he said he would be willing to back a play for me, provided I could find one, and that it was not too expensive to do. I found one, quickly enough—in fact, I already had my eye on it—called *The Dover Road*, and Mr. Ames advanced me the money for its production.

"*The Dover Road*, with which I made my bow as an independent producer, got off to a slow start, but within a matter of weeks it had become a smash hit. In practically no time at all, I was able to pay back all the money Mr. Ames had advanced toward its production.

"About this time, I married a glamorous young actress named Katharine Cornell and soon after acquired a home of my own on Beekman Place, New York.

"Looking back, one can easily see that my "entire future" did, indeed, depend upon 'that which I had written' back in June, 1913.

"By this time, I had long since lost track of my former Texas landlady. I always looked her up when possible, between my necessary trips outside of New York, but the last time I had been in touch with her was when I sent her tickets for A *Bill of Divorcement*, in which Katherine Cornell rose to stardom.

"After returning from an out-of-town business trip, I tried to reach Mrs. Heinsohn at the old Morningside Heights address but learned that she had moved away, leaving no forwarding address.

"I did *hear* from her again, under circumstances almost as peculiar as that first experience. It had been announced in the newspapers that I was going to produce *Jezebel*, with Tallulah Bankhead as star. Mrs. Heinsohn wrote me a note, urging me not to attempt it; she said, "Miss Bankhead will never play the role." And Miss Bankhead didn't! Tallulah had a severe illness that cancelled her out of the production. Rather than give it up, or postpone it indefinitely, I went ahead, substituting Miriam Hopkins in the role. *Jezebel* was a complete flop, one of the few real failures that I've ever had.

"The mysterious telephone message I received when we were on the verge of abandoning *The Barretts* came, of course, from Mrs. Heinsohn. She didn't give her name, but she didn't have to; and it was only a hunch that made me decide to answer the phone. She must have gone to considerable trouble to obtain my private telephone number, and by some devious device that I never knew about. And after delivering her message—'nothing to worry about'—she hung up, before I could ask her where she was living, or anything else. I have never seen her, or heard from her since.

"Anyway, we went ahead with our plans for producing *The Barretts*, and the rest is theatrical history.

"Superstition? Perhaps. But in the words of another producer, and a great mystic he was, too: 'There are more things in heaven and earth, Horatio . . .' You know the rest of it, of course."

BEATRICE LILLIE'S STORY

I recently interviewed Beatrice Lillie, backstage in her dressing room, for this book. Miss Lillie, as you know, is the internationally celebrated comedienne who in private life is Lady Peel.

"Well, I have an assortment of psychic experiences," Miss Lillie said. "For one thing, I have what you might call a personal poltergeist. It isn't destructive or unpleasant, but it *is* mischievous and has caused me quite a bit of embarrassment on several occasions.

"My poltergeist has been following me around for years," she went on, "but only started to get really annoying this winter, when I was appearing at the Palm Beach Playhouse in *An Evening with Beatrice Lillie*. As you may remember, there were several other people in my troupe, among them Constance Carpenter.

"Because I had more space in my dressing room, Connie preferred keeping one of her costumes there. No one had keys to the dressing room but myself and the maid, a young woman the theater had provided as a dresser, the daughter of some local Florida farm family.

"Well, at one performance, at the very last minute, Connie discovered that she couldn't get into her costume! The skirt had been stitched all the way across the hem, so that she couldn't step into it! She hastily ripped out the stitches and ran to the stage, and after that she kept the costume in her own dressing room.

"Of course we tried to find out who had done it, but we got nowhere. An odd thing: the stitches were very large ones, really basting stitches, in a coarse, yellowish cotton thread that no one around the theater had seen anywhere.

"In one of my numbers, in the second part of the show, I carry a small black fan. One evening, when I left my dressing-room for the number just before the one where I use the fan, it was lying on my dressing-room table. My dresser locked the dressing-room door, as usual, and accompanied me to the stage. When we returned, the fan was nowhere to be seen! We searched *everywhere*, but couldn't find it, and I finally had to go on with another fan that I located in my wardrobe trunk.

"Two days later, the fan was back on my dressing-room table, in exactly the same place we had last seen it. There was no possible way for it, at the time, to have been put back without someone seeing the person doing it!

"And in one of my numbers I wear a Japanese headdress, an elaborate black wig ornamented with tiny, decorative sticks securely fastened into the wig. One time I found the sticks had been removed and were lying in orderly fashion on my dressing-room table. Now, none of my friends would have thought it amusing to play such a disorganizing prank, even if they could have had access to my dressing-room; and certainly no one around the theater, including my maid, would have dreamed of playing such an unprofessional practical joke.

"But the time I *really* became annoyed was when one of my rings disappeared—again from my dressing table. I looked everywhere for it—everywhere that I could think of —then, almost as if it were a compulsion from some unknown source, finally stood on a chair and looked to see what might be on a high shelf in my dressing room. And there on the shelf it was!

"There have been a number of other manifestations, if that's the word for it, in my New York apartment, so I can't just blame the Palm Beach theater for housing such mischievous spirits.

"My sister Muriel, who lives in London, had several psychic experiences which might interest you. Muriel is the widow of the famous explorer, Arthur Weigall. Arthur was also a noted Egyptologist and visited Lord Carnarvon when the tomb of Tutankhamen was explored. As you know, there was supposed to be a curse that went with the tomb, or, rather, a curse on anyone who tampered with it. So, naturally, when Arthur Weigall died, the story was revived.

"I think it was with some idea of trying to contact her husband in the spirit world that my sister started going to séances and spiritualistic meetings, such as those sponsored by Hannen Swaffer, the British drama critic.

"But she wasn't really a gullible woman, as a couple of her experiences indicate. For instance, she was on the stage during one demonstration at Albert Hall, during which the medium was supposed to emit ectoplasm. Muriel broke all the rules by seizing the 'ectoplasm,' which turned out to be regurgitated cheesecloth! And she was promptly ejected from the hall!

"On another occasion, my sister invited a medium to her own home. The woman worked with a trumpet—in the dark of course—and at one point Muriel, who sat facing her, their knees almost touching, began to suspect that the woman was manipulating the trumpet. Muriel suddenly leaned forward and seized both of the woman's hands, whereupon the trumpet, which had been standing on the floor, leaped about four feet into the air, and fell with a clatter at their feet.

"The medium must have been just as surprised as my sister, for both women fainted dead away!"

...AND OTHER
THEATRICAL SPOOKS

Noel Coward had a ghost, too; one that occasionally walked through the floor-length window into the living room of his studio in the old Chelsea quarter of London. He told me that he had never seen it himself, although some of his friends had, many times. But he didn't deny that this ghostly intruder inspired him to write *Blithe Spirit*, in which a similar ghostly entrance occurs.

Perhaps like Bea Lillie, Noel's familiar is a "personal poltergeist," for since he sold his London home and moved to Bermuda, he has complained of being haunted in his new quarters at Spithead Lodge, in Warwick Parish.

When Alexander Woollcott died, his co-operative apartment on East 52nd Street was bought by Coward and occupied by him until the beginning of World War II. Perhaps Noel brought along his own special aura, to add to that of Woollcott. Among the owners who have succeeded him since, another theatrical producer, Arnold Saint-Subber, tells me that the most unaccountable things happened to his books during his occupancy there! Woollcott, an autocrat in such matters, probably didn't approve of Saint-Subber's choice of reading matter!

IDA LUPINO'S STORY

Hollywood supplied me with a surprising number of good stories along supernatural lines.

Paul Coates, a columnist for the Los Angeles *Mirror-News*, who has another story of his own elsewhere in this book, told me that he and his wife (the former Renée DeMarco) occupied the three-story former carriage house on the estate of one of the early California millionaires and were so plagued by the unexplainable goings-on there that they were finally impelled to move.

Paul, a firm disbeliever in such things, said that most of the spirit activities, or whatever they were, seemed to be concentrated on the top floor. This was originally used as quarters for the maid for their three children, but after the maid left because of the nocturnal disturbances, Paul took it over for his own den. But even he couldn't take it, and lost so much needed sleep because of the eerie noises that he closed up the room and moved his lares and penates elsewhere.

Walter Pidgeon told me, quite casually, while we were together on a junket to Rio de Janeiro, that he had a supernatural story of his own—something that took place a long time ago, when he was a small boy in Canada.

Among his playmates were twins—Bobby and Billy, we'll have to call them—children of one of the neighbors. On one occasion when Walter was in their house he asked the boys' mother to get him a drink of water, and followed her into the kitchen. One of the twins, Billy, was home, but the other, Bobby, was out skating.

The mother had drawn a glass of water from the faucet and handed it to Walter. Suddenly she cried out, "Oh, not

Bobby!" and fainted away, falling to the floor. Almost before she could be revived, a phone call came saying that Bobby had fallen through the ice and drowned.

Ida Lupino's story, also involving a telephone call, was even more dramatic.

"My father belonged to a club in London similar to the Lambs Club in New York," Ida wrote me. "He had the title of Treasurer of Secrets, which carries with it Masonic responsibilities. The story involves a fellow member, and one of his closest friends, to whom I shall have to give the fictitious name of Andrew Meyer, for a variety of reasons.

" 'Uncle Andy,' as I called him, was a frequent visitor at our home and I was very fond of him; in fact, all of us were.

"At the time, we were living with my grandmother at her home in the outskirts of London, while my parents—whom I always called by their first names, Stanley and Connie— were playing an engagement in one of the London variety houses.

"One night, about half past ten, I woke up and couldn't go back to sleep again. I had had a disturbing dream about Uncle Andy and decided to go downstairs and tell my grandmother about it. I was nine years old and very impressionable at the time.

"Granny was in the kitchen, preparing supper for my parents, who were due back from the theater where they were working. While I was telling Granny about my dream, the phone in the hall rang.

" 'Answer it, Ida,' Granny said. 'I have my hands full.'

"I went to the phone, took the receiver off the hook and heard a voice on the line, but it was so faint that I could scarcely understand the words. Finally, the voice became stronger and I could understand the message, repeated monotonously several times: 'I must talk to Stanley. It is terribly important.'

"I answered: 'Oh, it's you, Uncle Andy! Daddy isn't home yet.' But the voice kept repeating the same words, and this time quite distinctly: 'Stanley—I must talk to Stanley— it's terribly important.'

"I asked him to hold the line until I could get Granny. She went to the phone and I heard her say, 'Why, Andy—

51

are you *ill?* I'll ask Stanley to call you the moment he comes in.' Then the phone was cut off and there was no further talk.

"Grandmother was quite cross. She flashed the switchboard operator and told her that a phone call had been interrupted. She was even more exasperated when the operator said she didn't believe there had been a call on the line during the past hour. There being no way to complete the call—she didn't know from what part of London Uncle Andy had been phoning—she went back to her chores.

"About half an hour later, Stanley and Connie arrived home and I gave Stanley Uncle Andy's message. Connie dropped suddenly into a chair and looked as though she were going to faint.

"Stanley said I must be mistaken—and, anyway, it was time for me to be in bed.

"Granny said, 'But she's *not* mistaken, Stanley, and I think you had better call Andy. He sounded as though he was very ill.'

" 'Mom—' Stanley answered, and I'll never forget how tense his voice sounded, 'Andrew Meyer is dead. He hung himself three days ago.' "

JACK BARAGWANATH'S STORY

Nothing fascinates students of the occult more than the phenomenon called a *poltergeist.* That's a German word for a frisky, mischievous or obstreperous type of spirit that specializes in moving objects, hurling things around and, above all, in throwing stones. The stones apparently come from nowhere. Hereward Carrington, in collaboration with psychoanalyst Nandor Fodor, turned out a book on this particular kind of "spookery," entitled *Haunted People: Story of the Poltergeist Down the Centuries* (F. P. Dutton & Co., 1951).

Dr. Carrington differentiates the poltergeist in this way: while ordinary ghosts haunt houses, or places, the poltergeist haunts people. His book lists 375 typical poltergeist cases, of which 330 never could be explained. The cases come from every part of the globe and range from the year 355 A.D. to 1949.

As near as anyone can come to a conclusion about this species of haunting is that undirected and irresponsible forces, outside the human body, *but emanating from it,* are responsible. The preponderance of them are associated in some way with birth or pregnancy, but more particularly with puberty. Young children, and especially young girls, seem to be bothered most.

It was a group of adolescent girls who started the witchcraft trials in Salem, and I think a modern student of supernatural phenomena would have put up a sign in the court room reading *Poltergeists at Work.*

Poltergeist manifestations usually end just as abruptly—and as mysteriously—as they start.

Jack Baragwanath is the only person I know who has had an experience that could clearly be recognized as that of a poltergeist at work—the destructive, rock-throwing kind.

Jack—his full name is John G. Baragwanath, a celebrated mining engineer whose wife was the late Neysa McMein—

spent a number of years knocking around the wildest parts of Chile and Peru, in the course of which he had many extraordinary and dramatic experiences. The Andean scene, he says, lends itself especially to the weird and unearthly, and one adventure stands out in his mind today because he could never find any logical explanation for it.

"When I was twenty-seven," Jack told me, "my firm sent me to a village in central Peru, where I was to take temporary charge of a small but very rich copper mine.

"One day, Father Condé, a French priest with whom I had become acquainted, came to see me in quite a flustered state. He said he wanted to discuss with me something strange that was going on in the town.

"Several days before, an Indian named Vasquez begged him to come to his home and exorcise the spirits that had taken possession of the place and were driving him and his family frantic. For a week or more, it seems, the members of his household had been repeatedly struck by stones thrown by unseen hands *while inside the house.* This sometimes happened during the day but more frequently at night, when the doors were closed and the shutters securely bolted.

"The Indian, Vasquez, was worked up to a great pitch of excitement and it was obvious that something really disturbing was going on. So Father Condé paid the family a visit, but his presence failed to dissipate the trouble. The strange visitations persisted, and he admitted that he was completely baffled.

"The situation interested me very much, so I suggested that we go and call on the Vasquez family together. The priest suggested that we go immediately, so we set out. On the way to town, we encountered the mayor, explained the circumstances and asked if he would like to accompany us. He agreed to go.

"We went directly to the house, which was a one-story affair of adobe brick, roofed over with a rough, native tile. There was a combination living room and kitchen, a bedroom and a storeroom. The rooms were sealed with *tucullo,* a kind of unbleached cotton goods.

"The family consisted of Vasquez, his wife and three girls, ranging from eight to fifteen years of age. The mother was in a hysterical condition. Her face and hands were covered with bumps and scars, and the girls also had many bruises.

"They showed us a pile of rocks, ranging in size from pebbles to cobblestones, and there were also pieces of broken tile and lumps of hard, dried mud. These, the mother said, had been thrown at them during the past ten days. Oddly, none of these objects had struck Vasquez himself, nor had any of the family been struck while *outside the house.*

"We inspected the premises carefully, then took a chair from the living room and placed it in the center of the almost empty storeroom. Then we persuaded one of the daughters, the middle child—an intelligent-looking girl of about twelve—to sit on it. The girl's head and face were badly bruised and cut.

"We closed the heavy door leading to the living room and then the three of us—the priest, the mayor and I—stood shoulder to shoulder in the doorway, with our backs against the door.

"The girl sat in the center of the room, facing us. Behind her was a window with four small panes, set in a deep frame in the wall. The window, which gave onto the street, was nailed tightly shut, and there was no other opening into the room. We examined the walls carefully, also the ceiling and the hard mud floor. There was no place where any person, or any large object, could possibly be concealed.

"We stood there, tense and expectant, for some time. Nothing happened and after about twenty minutes our gaze, which had been fixed on the girl, may have wandered. (I mention this to allow for any benefit of doubt about what happened.)

"Suddenly, we heard a noise like a dull slap, followed by a thud. Then we saw, rolling across the floor, away from the girl, a stone about as large as a man's two fists. The stone had struck the girl on the cheek, with enough force to jerk her sideways, though not hard enough to knock her off the chair.

"The girl burst into sobs, but remained seated on the chair. The priest and I stayed where we were, but the mayor
55

rushed over to the stone, in great excitement, and picked it up.

" 'There is some terrible fake going on here!' he shouted. 'That must be a false window.' And with that, he threw the stone at the window, smashing it to bits.

"Keeping the door closed, we went over the walls and ceiling of the room, inch by inch, trying to find a place through which the stone might have been thrown. But there was no opening of any kind.

"The girl had been hit on the cheek, so the stone would have had to come from one side of the room. All three of us could have sworn that there had been no stones on the floor, and if that girl had had it concealed on her person she would have to be a sleight-of-hand artist.

"From the sound of the thud and the effect of the blow, it appeared to have been thrown underhand from a distance of about six feet. It could not possibly have come from the ceiling or from either the window or the door, even if these apertures had been opened. We were completely baffled.

"The little girl's cheek was beginning to swell and we did what we could to soothe her. While the mayor and Father Condé remained with the family, I went out and bought some beer for the father and mother and some trinkets for the girls. When we left them, they were at least as happy as they could be, under the circumstances.

"I followed the case carefully. The mysterious attacks kept up for about a week more, and then stopped just as suddenly as they had begun.

"I wouldn't be surprised if anyone disbelieved this story because I can hardly believe it myself, but I am telling it exactly as it happened. For years I have tried to find some explanation for what went on, but I am no nearer a solution today than I was at the time."

STUART CLOETE'S STORY

Since Africa is the "dark continent," where voodoo doctors still practice their strange arts, and all sorts of weird and unexplainable things are said to happen, I felt sure I would get a good story out of Stuart Cloete, who is himself descended from the Boers and has spent a number of years in Capetown. Cloete is probably best known for his classic and dramatic story, *Turning Wheels*, but he has also written several important books on Africa, the latest being *The African Giant*.

I did get a good story out of him, but it had nothing to do with Africa!

"It happened in Wyoming," Stuart told me. "We—Tiny and I (Tiny being my pet name for my wife, Rehna)—were staying with Struthers Burt at his Jackson Hole ranch. Early one evening, eight of us—Tiny, myself, Struthers and his wife, Katherine Newlin Burt, Margaret Reed, and some others whose names I have forgotten—went for a picnic at a spot not far from his ranch. It was a lovely place beside a mountain stream, which we reached by a narrow, winding path.

"We had lighted a big fire on which to broil our steaks and make coffee, and as twilight descended our fire was the only light we had in the growing darkness.

"We were seated on the path that followed the stream, chatting, when I heard the sound of a galloping horse. The hoofbeats came nearer and nearer, and so rapidly that there would hardly be time to get out of the way if the horse were coming up the path. I couldn't see a thing, but the feeling was so vivid that the horse *was* racing up the path, at breakneck speed, that I automatically ducked my head when it seemed that the horse had reached the spot where I would be in his way. *And Tiny and two others in the party also ducked their heads at the same time!*

57

"Four members of the party heard it, four didn't, yet the sound was loud enough to be heard by everyone present. It was exactly that of a horse racing ahead, then halting momentarily in order to jump *over* an object. Once over the object—our heads, in this instance—the horse seemed to race on up the path, until the sound of the hoofbeats disappeared. It all happened so suddenly and dramatically that we were all a little breathless from the experience.

"We all continued to talk about the incident, for days afterward. Possibly as a clue to the mystery, Struthers told me something about the background of the country. The region had been quite lawless; there was a sort of 'Deadman's Gulch' atmosphere about the whole area. There was a log cabin nearby which was peppered with bullet holes, and one of the local legends was that a man, prospecting for alluvial gold in the stream where we held our picnic, had been murdered. It was easy to imagine either the murderer taking off with his stolen gold, or someone galloping back to report the crime, astride that ghostly horse.

"As I said before, we *saw* nothing; but we not only heard the galloping horse but actually felt the vibrations of the hoof beats. In fact, the *ground shook*. It couldn't have been just a matter of acoustics, because there were no highways or other paths nearby, and the surrounding region was quite thickly wooded."

Rehna Cloete, Stuart Cloete's wife, who spent eight years in Africa with her husband and recently incorporated her own experiences into a very amusing and informative book called *The Nylon Safari*, had plenty to say about the weird and unexplainable things that go on in Africa. Of how the photographs she took in a "juju" hut failed to come out, though every other picture on the same camera film was perfect (it is one of the African legends that white men cannot photograph any of these forbidden objects) and about a "ghost tree" that she, and only she, saw.

"We bought ourselves a dear little house in Stranvskloof, about a hundred miles from Capetown, located in a valley surrounded by mountains," as Rehna tells it. "The area had once been noted for its trees, huge and very old yellowwood trees that might be compared to the redwood trees of California for size and age.

"These yellowwood trees had been enormous and they grew approximately straight, for which reason they had been used as beams and floor boards in many of the older houses in the Capetown area. But by now the area was practically denuded; only small trees, eight or ten feet high, grew there.

"One day I was in the garden, helping Stuart, when I wandered off to a nearby area where I had never been before. And there, right in my path, was a huge and beautiful tree —*an enormous tree!*

"I rushed back to tell Stuart. He was skeptical; 'Why haven't we seen it before?' he wanted to know. I decided the best thing to do was to have him see it for himself, so I persuaded him to go back with me to the spot. I was prepared to point it out triumphantly and say, 'There—see for yourself!' But when I got back to the spot in the woods where I had been before, the tree wasn't there! There wasn't a sign or suggestion of a big tree! And I had stood under it, looked up into its branches, reveled in the thought that one of these forest giants had been spared!

"My memory of it was so vivid that I could describe it accurately to Stuart. He decided that it was a *podocarpus,* or yellowwood tree, such as had once existed in profusion in this valley but had disappeared long ago.

"And I have another story for your collection, of a quite different sort," Rehna continued. "This was something that happened to me when I was a child of about six, living with my grandparents in Pennsylvania.

"My grandmother had taken me along when she went to spend the day visiting an elderly friend. After lunch, I was taken to a bedroom for a nap; the shades were drawn and I was left alone.

"I think I must have dozed off, but I was certainly wide awake when I first noticed a full-length pier-glass mirror, on a tilted stand. In the rather dim light of the room, to which my eyes were by now accustomed, I saw a sort of foggy reflection in the mirror.

"As I continued to watch the mirror, the images in it became clearer and I distinctly made out the shadows, or reflections, of a man and a woman, *moving.* A terrific struggle seemed to be going on between them. I cried out in terror and my screams were heard by my grandmother.

"When Grandmother came into the room, the images disappeared, but not suddenly; they seemed to sort of flicker out, and it was quite a few seconds before the glass was clear again.

"My grandmother quieted me down and took me home. None of my family believed my story, of course, but I remembered it very well, and as I grew older I became determined to try to trace something of the history of both the house and its furnishings.

"One thing I did learn to my satisfaction: that mirror had once been in a house in Ireland in which a murder had taken place. By now, it was only legendary, but the supposition was that a man had strangled his wife there.

"The experience was so vivid in my mind that for years I couldn't sleep in a room with a mirror, and even today mirrors have a morbidly strange fascination for me, especially in certain lights. I think I must have a subconscious fear that if I look too long into them, I will see things that weren't intended for me to see!"

MABEL MERCER'S STORY

I was on my way uptown from the National Arts Club, where Stuart Cloete had told me the story of the galloping ghost horse, when I dropped in at the Byline Room to see Mabel Mercer about doing a column profile on her. I didn't expect to get a spooky story here, but I did!

"I can still shut my eyes and hear the sound of those marching feet," Mabel said, with a slight shudder. "It happened when I was fifteen years old, but it is just as vivid to me today as if it had happened yesterday!"

"Marching feet?" I inquired.

"Yes. I was in Glasgow, Scotland, making my debut in show business in a vaudeville act with my aunt. During a layoff there, my aunt and I were invited to dine at the home of a Mrs. S., who lived in a suburb of Glasgow, a residential quarter something like Gramercy Park in New York.

"This was in 1915. The British Empire had been at war nearly a year, and one saw evidences of it on almost all sides, but there was nothing in this quiet residential neighborhood to remind us of it.

"Our hostess lived in a large, old-fashioned house that had a wide front hall; the hall was so large, in fact, that it boasted a fireplace. The only piece of furniture I can remember was a huge and particularly heavy oak table, possibly six feet long, with massive, turned legs. The floor was carpeted, or there were heavy rugs, I don't remember which, but in any case the floor was well-padded—there is a point to this.

"We had had a leisurely dinner, with coffee afterward in the sitting room. It was nearly ten o'clock and we were about to take our leave when our hostess remarked that she must post a letter to her husband. He was with the British Army, though where he was located and what he was doing were top secret, even to her.

"The night outside was balmy, for Scotland, and Mrs. S. suggested that we walk with her to the nearest post box, which I believe was about a block away. We, the three of us, were about to go out of the front door when we heard the sound of marching feet, a sound that is immediately recognizable by anyone who has ever been near marching troops—a rhythmic, scuffling step that is unmistakable.

"Mrs. S. seemed quite surprised since, so far as she knew, no troops were stationed in Glasgow at the time, or at least not in this immediate vicinity. As she was commenting on this, the sound grew louder and louder, as if the troops were growing nearer.

"The three of us rushed outside to see the soldiers pass and were astonished to find everything quiet out of doors, not a sight or *sound* of marching troops, or anything out of the ordinary to disturb the quiet of that suburban neighborhood.

"Quite baffled, we went back into the house and had an even greater surprise: the sound of marching troops was still going on, louder than before; in fact, almost deafening! And the vibration of marching feet *actually shook the floor!* Even the heavy oak table was quivering.

"We stood there, absolutely petrified with bewilderment, yes, and *fear*. Gradually, the sound began to diminish, and it continued to diminish until it finally died away in the distance, exactly as it does when a regiment of soldiers has passed out of sight and sound.

"Mrs. S. suggested that we accompany her down the street, to try to locate a policeman and ask if he could explain it. We did locate one, several blocks away. Mrs. S. asked him if he knew of any troop movements in this vicinity. He said that he knew of none—certainly none that had passed his way on this particular evening, and he had been on duty for several hours.

"I was in Glasgow some time later and called on Mrs. S., thinking she might have cleared up the mystery. But she evidently was away at the time; at any rate, the house was closed and I never saw her again.

"I wonder what, if anything, the letter she had written to her husband, and was about to post, had to do with it!"

Though Mabel Mercer hadn't heard of it, the Highland Scots have a word, *taradh*, that has been described by some writers as "an influence exerted unconsciously by the strong wishes on the part of a person at a distance, to which they attribute such phenomena as the sound of *viewless* feet that pass."

In the light of this definition, perhaps Mrs. S.'s letter to her husband *did* have something to do with what went on that evening in Glasgow; perhaps her thoughts, or possibly his thoughts, had bridged the distance between them.

GORDON BARROWS' STORY

One interesting angle about contemporary experiences in the supernormal is that many of them parallel historical incidents. Take the story of Goethe, the German poet, and compare it with the story told me by Gordon Barrows, who incidentally had never heard the Goethe legend.

Goethe wrote that while traveling down a particular road on horseback he became aware of a companion riding alongside him. Without glancing directly at the stranger, he could still take in all the details of the clothing he wore, which was strikingly different from his own. As he continued to ride along, he became uncomfortably aware that the silent and unbidden companion was *himself*. Eight years *later*, Goethe found himself riding along the same road, again on horseback, and this time attired in the identical costume that he had seen on the stranger.

The apparition that Gordon Barrows met on a wild winter night in a Wyoming canyon was wearing the identical jacket that he himself had worn three years *before* during World War II.

Barrows is the thirty-two-year-old managing editor of the *World Petroleum* magazine, located at 604 Fifth Avenue, New York. Prior to taking over that position, he was a foreign representative for the Standard Oil Company of California.

"In April of 1946, I got out of the Army and went home to the family ranch near Cody, Wyoming," Barrows writes. "Near the end of that summer I went to California to visit my sister.

"We received notice of a sale of army equipment, with preference given to ex-GI's. At my dad's request, I went down to Oceanside, California, to attend the sale, and bought a jeep.

"At the beginning of the college term that fall, I went

back to the University of Wyoming at Laramie to finish my bachelor's degree. All winter long I had been thinking how nice it would be to have the jeep to run around in on the campus and when spring vacation came, I decided to go home and get it. I went to our ranch near Cody, which was about five hundred miles away, and, despite the family's protests, got the jeep and started back.

"It wasn't a very sensible thing to do, if you know Wyoming weather. We've been known to have bad snowstorms as late as May, and this was March. The jeep was completely open, but I bundled myself up in an old parka, with lined boots and mittens, and set out. I knew I couldn't make much time with the jeep, so I started early in the morning. It was bitterly cold, and the parka wasn't much protection from the wind.

"The road to Laramie goes through long stretches of desolate country. From Shoshone to Thermopolis is a hundred-mile stretch, with only a couple of country stores on the route, and other stretches are just as deserted. It took me five hours to get to Thermopolis, and another four, with a stopover for lunch, to reach Casper, about 250 miles farther—the halfway point.

"I was averaging only about thirty-five miles per hour; there was snow on the road, and I realized that if I were going to get to Laramie in time for Monday classes I couldn't linger along the route. I was sleepy by then, and the sun was setting, but I was determined to go on.

"To make things worse, it started to snow. Out of Casper, the road is straight and narrow. At first it passes through some oil-well country where there are a couple of refineries and company installations; as it goes toward Torrington it grows quite desolate. By now the snow was getting heavier, fogging my windshield, so I had to drive with one hand, using the other one to work the manual windshield wiper.

"After leaving Torrington, there is a fork where the road divides. One road goes to Cheyenne (Wyoming's largest city—about thirty thousand population) and there are some small towns along the way. The right road goes to Laramie, through Telephone Canyon. From the base of the canyon to the seven-thousand-foot plateau on which Laramie is located there isn't a house or a ranch, or any sign of human habitation.

"As I drove through the night, pumping the windshield

wiper with my mittened hand, my headlight picked up red lights ahead—lights of cars stalled in the whirling snow, which by now was becoming a blizzard. I drew up to the cars and discovered one was a Greyhound bus, nearly off the road because the driver couldn't see his way. Another was a police car. The patrolman was talking to the bus driver when I stopped and got out.

" 'Nobody has been through,' I heard him saying, 'and nobody is going through. Road's closed through the canyon.' Then, as I stepped up, he added, 'Weather report says there's already four inches of snow and more coming. If anybody got stuck in that canyon they might be there for a week before another car came through, and there's no ranch where you could get help.'

"I said nothing; just took off toward the canyon entrance. Except for the bus lights, which were pretty dim, you could see nothing. The fork of the road that led into the canyon was completely under snow and there wasn't a car track, indicating that nobody had passed that way since the blizzard started. Very few cars used it even in good weather, because the road was narrow in places, winding through the gorge, with drops of hundreds of feet, and no stone fences to stop a car from going over.

"There were lots of car tracks on the Cheyenne fork, and I walked back to the jeep, trying to make up my mind. If I didn't get through now, I wouldn't be able to get through for a couple of days; I would have to stay in Casper, or go on to Cheyenne and get held up there. I determined to go through, even though it was an utterly foolhardy decision, considering the weather.

"I backed the jeep around and went back toward Casper. About a quarter of a mile away I stopped, turned off the lights, and waited. I saw the bus slowly lumbering off up the Cheyenne fork and watched the police car follow, a little later. I waited a little longer, then put the jeep in four-wheel drive and started up the right fork. When the other cars were far enough away not to see me, I turned on the headlights.

"It was about eleven o'clock by now and the snow was still coming down. I was having no trouble getting through the snow because of the four-wheel drive, but I was so tired from eighteen hours of non-stop driving, and so numb from the cold, that I had to slap my face occasionally to keep awake.

"The jeep was coming to the entrance of the canyon now and there was a long hill, quite straight, sloping down to the entrance. As I topped the hill and came down the road, nearly a quarter of a mile, I saw a man walking ahead of me. He was on the left side of the road, and as I drove down toward him I was surprised to see that he wasn't even wearing a warm parka.

"In Wyoming, you don't pass by anyone in a situation like that. I knew there was no ranch, or any other place, to stop at for the thirty-five miles of the canyon—and quite a distance beyond that. The way the man was dressed, he might easily die on the road from exposure.

"I stopped about twenty-five feet away and waited. He turned around and came up to my car, on the left side of the road—on the side where I sat behind the steering wheel. When he got in range of the headlights, I saw that he was dressed in a light jacket, such as I had worn myself in the Army, something called a Tank Corps jacket, with elastic cuffs and the same elastic material at the neck. And it immediately occurred to me, without any astonishment— probably because I was almost numb from the cold and lack of sleep—that *he looked exactly like me*. Somehow, though, this odd coincidence seemed the most natural thing in the world.

"He walked steadily up to the car, through the headlights, and came right to me.

" 'You look sleepy,' he said. 'Want *me* to drive?'

" 'Thanks,' I said, and moved over without another word. Then he got behind the wheel.

A jeep has a small back seat that folds up. I folded it up and lay down between the two front seats, with my knees on the right-hand front seat and my head resting on the cold metal of the back floor. I remember my head bumping on the floor as the jeep bounced along in the snow.

"The next thing I remember, I was waking up. The jeep had stopped and the driver was sitting motionless behind the wheel. I sat up, brushing the parka back from my eyes. The engine wasn't on, and there wasn't a sound, except for the howling of some coyotes in the distance. The snow had stopped and the stars were out, clear and bright. Off to the right were lights, and I knew that they came from the only ranch at the Laramie end of the canyon. While I was asleep on the floor, we had driven *the entire length of Telephone Canyon!*

"We were now on top of the last hill, looking down. Beyond the base of the hill the road straightens out and runs for forty miles, as straight as a string, to Laramie.

"My passenger got out of the jeep. I looked at him and asked something about whether he wanted to go on into Laramie.

" 'No thanks,' he said, and started to turn away.

" 'Well, thanks a lot,' I said.

" 'You're welcome,' he answered.

"I got behind the wheel, started the engine, and drove down the hill a way. A few feet along, I stopped and turned to wave to my companion of the night. But he had turned his back on me and was walking back the way we had come —back into the canyon, where I had picked him up.

"I felt good, quite rested, and the rest of the drive was easy, the road being straight ahead, with very little snow. I drove into Laramie, got a room and slept all day.

"The whole experience, somehow, had seemed perfectly natural, and I wouldn't have thought much about it if someone hadn't asked me a couple of days later if I had driven alone through Telephone Canyon on that particular night.

" 'Sure!' I answered, and then, as an afterthought, added; 'Come to think about it, I didn't drive *all* the way by myself. I picked up a hitch-hiker who spelled me at the wheel through Telephone Canyon.'

" 'You were lucky,' my friend said. 'I had to stay in Casper until I could get through.'

" 'You know,' I said, musingly, as the experience began to come back to me, 'there *was* something funny about it: the hitch-hiker was walking on that stretch of road on the Casper side of the canyon, wearing nothing but a Tank Corps jacket. And he got out after we left the canyon and walked back into it.

" 'Into the *canyon?*' my friend asked, incredulously. 'That's impossible! He couldn't have lasted in there more than a couple of hours.'

" 'And, come to think of it,' I added thoughtfully, 'he looked exactly *like* me!'

"I got such a peculiar look from my friend that I never told the story again; have never told it, in fact, until just now, ten years after it happened.

"At the time, the experience seemed the most natural thing in the world—like in a dream in which preposterous things seem ordinary.

"To this day, the memory of the experience is sharp and exact, every detail of it. I could go back to Telephone Canyon right now, and show you the spot where I picked up the hitch-hiker, as well as the spot where I let him off."

MARY WOOD'S STORY

We do hear spook stories in the oddest places!

It was while on a chartered bus returning from Nottingham, England, where we had gone in connection with some movie junket, that this story came to me from Mary Wood, the pretty and talented editor for radio and television on the Cincinnati *Post*.

I don't know what brought it up, unless it was because the day before we had both enjoyed a personally conducted tour of Hampton Court, where Henry VIII made so much personal history. The guide had voluntarily regaled us with stories of the ghost of Katherine Howard, the unhappy girl who was that monarch's fifth wife. The guide told us that Katherine can still be heard racing down the hall and pounding on the door of Henry's chapel before the guards captured her, kicking and screaming, and led her off to further imprisonment and eventual execution.

"I have a ghost story of my own," Mary mused, "though not like that," she hastened to add.

"I remember it vividly now, although it made very little impression on me at the time. I was very young then—seven, as I recall—and I suppose children accept such things as a matter of course; there are so many things they don't understand at the time.

"In those days I was living with my mother and grandmother in a rambling old house in New Orleans, on Valence Street, just off St. Charles Avenue.

"I suppose I was fond of my mother, but today she is just a dim recollection; it is my grandmother who stands out in my memory. She was my whole world: I adored her, and I vividly remember so many things about her: her fascinating stories of New Orleans during the Civil War; her humor and great understanding; the delicate odor of perfume—parma violets, I think it was—that always seemed to cling to her.

70

We were practically inseparable, even shared the same old-fashioned double bed, which was covered by a tester from which hung voluminous folds of white mosquito netting.

"Grandmother was one of a large family that had lived in the Mississippi Delta. My great-grandfather, who was a wealthy sugar plantation owner up to the war, sired twenty children. Of all her many sisters, my grandmother's favorite was Ida, several years her senior. Aunt Ida, whom Grandmother always called 'Sister Ida,' was now living on a plantation near Lake Charles, Louisiana, and although they visited back and forth frequently, they also indulged in an old southern custom of writing each other *every day*.

"As I remember, Grandmother had just returned from a visit to Aunt Ida when, several nights later, Aunt Ida paid her last visit to *us*—from the spirit world.

"It must have been past midnight when I was awakened by my grandmother's voice. She was sitting up in bed, talking to someone who was invisible to me. Whoever it was apparently was standing at the foot of our bed. There must have been moonlight streaming into the room because I remember exactly how Grandmother looked. She was wearing her customary night attire—a long cambric nightgown with high ruffled neck and long sleeves, and, of course, her beruffled and beribboned nightcap.

"It was evident that Grandmother wasn't frightened or upset; merely very sad. I could hear only her end of the conversation, but I soon realized that she was talking to Aunt Ida and that Aunt Ida was requesting her to do certain things.

" 'Yes, Sister Ida; I understand,' I can remember hearing Grandmother saying. 'You want Ida May to have your garnet cross and the paisley shawl.'

"There were other instructions, but that particular one stands out in my memory because Ida May was my mother and she, in turn, left the garnet cross to me.

"Grandmother and Aunt Ida must have talked for about ten minutes. Then the time came for them to say good-by. Only then did tears begin to stream down my grandmother's lovely face.

" 'Good-by, Sister Ida,' she said. 'I shall miss you very much.'

"Then she lay back in bed and told me, quietly and unemotionally, that Aunt Ida had just passed away and had

71

come to say good-by. I don't recall being frightened in the least, just sleepy.

"Next morning the telegram came telling of Aunt Ida's death from a heart attack. She had passed away, rather suddenly, just before midnight."

WILLIAM SLOANE'S STORY

"When I admitted to you over the phone the other day that I once spent some nights in a haunted house, it was not with the idea of whetting your interest in a possible story!"

Thus spoke Mr. William Sloane, Director of the Rutgers University Press at New Brunswick, New Jersey, and a neighbor of mine in Rockland County, New York, whom I had called about a wholly different matter. This book being very much on my mind at the moment, however, I mentioned it to him and found that, naturally, he too had a story!

"The experience itself was far less dramatic than the expressions on the faces of those to whom I have described it," writes Mr. Sloane.

"To profess to a belief that some houses are haunted, and to confess to having had a personal experience in one of them, isn't considered intellectually respectable, so I am always a little sorry to unsettle my friends by such a confession; sorrier, still, to reveal that, in the final analysis, I am compelled to believe in the evidence of my senses, which once in a while turn in such a nonscientific report.

"Here's the story:

"Some years ago I was president of my own small New York publishing house. Its affairs fell upon precarious days and, in an attempt to find solutions for its difficulties, it became necessary to spend several nights a week working late in New York City, too late to catch the last train for my home in Rockland County.

"Some of my friends knew about this situation and one, also a publisher, suggested that I rent her house for the summer, while she was spending some months abroad with her children. I explained that my expense account didn't include money for house rent.

" 'Money's not the point,' she replied. 'You can rent the whole place for twenty-five dollars a month.'

73

" 'That's ridiculous,' I told her. 'You have a four-story house on a good street on the upper East side. The town is crawling with people who want summer rentals such as you have to offer.'

"She hesitated a moment, then said: 'Well, you're something of a friend of the family. I'd *like* you to have it. I got it myself at a real bargain, and if you'll stay in it, I won't have the expense of having it looked after while I'm gone.'

" 'You wouldn't, with *really* paying tenants, either,' I pointed out.

" 'No,' she said, 'but actually I don't *want* to rent it to just anyone. You take the place for the three months that I'm gone. I'll lock up the house and send you the keys from my office, the first of the month.'

"That's how it was arranged.

"I packed some sheets and towels into a suitcase and went around to the house soon after my landlady departed for Europe. The house was one of those ugly, sturdily-built mansions that solid New York citizens built for themselves in the years between 1900 and 1915. It was of brick and stone, with a bow window on the street, a stoop going up to the front door, with the conventional foyer, and the usual interior floor plan.

"Downstairs, in the half-basement, was a furnace room and storage and servants' space. On the main floor, a large living room on the street side, a dining room behind it, and a kitchen on an ell extending into the back yard. On the floor above there were two master bedrooms, a dressing room and a large bath in the center of the house. The top floor contained two smaller rooms, a bath, a hall and a double bedroom.

"The main stairway started in the front hall and ascended toward the back of the house. The door to the real master bedroom on the third floor—the room I had picked out for my own occupancy—was almost opposite the head of this flight of stairs (it's rather important to this story to keep this in mind). The hall then ran toward the front of the house, and the final flight of stairs to the top floor ascended from it and toward the rear. When my landlady's family was in residence, the top floor was devoted to the children.

"As I recall it, I reached the house very late this first night, a Monday evening, and I was tired to the bone. Tired as I was, however, I decided to take out the flashlight that I usually carried in my briefcase and check the doors and windows on the two lower floors. I then went up to the master bedroom, hauled forth my sheets, made the bed and fell instantly into a dreamless and uninterrupted sleep.

"Not so the second night! On Tuesday, I arrived at the place after dinner, with several manuscripts under my arm. Once again, I made the rounds of the two lower floors. Frankly, I admitted to myself, I wished I hadn't taken the place: a whole house seemed too much of a good thing. Burglary is common enough in the city, and while my presence would make the place appear occupied a part of the time, it would be dark and empty more often than not—an ideal target, I thought, for breaking and entering.

"After turning a good many lights on and off, and browsing among the bookshelves, I returned to my manuscripts, which I intended to read in bed.

"The evening was fiercely hot, so I took off all my clothes and didn't bother with pajamas. I also left the door onto the stairs and hall open, in the hope of some small amount of breeze through the rooms. I read for an hour or so, then switched off the light and lay back to think about the problems confronting me. In perhaps five minutes, I heard the sound of footsteps coming up the stairs, apparently those of a man. The tread was firm and regular; not at all the step of someone coming up a dark staircase, unless it were a person completely familiar with the house.

"The steadiness of the steps reassured me, at first. No burglar would make that much noise. I snatched for the top sheet, turned on the headboard reading light over the bed and called out that most clichéd of all phrases: 'Who's there?'

"There was no reply, but the steps stopped. I plunged into my pajama bottoms, picked up the flashlight, and strode into the hall, shining the light in front of me. The light had a good, strong beam and I could see clear down to the front door. There was no one there.

"To be quite honest, I wasn't enjoying myself at this moment, and it was only after some self-exhortation that I decided to go over the whole house again. I did, and I found everything locked tight, including all the windows except the one in my bedroom.

"The following morning, I went over the place again, paying particular attention to the architectural structure of the house. Those stairs were, so far as I could tell without tearing off the panelling, of the best construction. I went up and down them, trying to locate any possible sound of treads or beams springing back into position. There was no such sound. Indeed, for the rest of that summer, I never heard any of the usual night noises that I, like everyone else, grow accustomed to in a house, whether it is in the city or in the country.

"On Thursday, which was my next night to spend in the city, I took back to the house, in addition to the manuscripts, a pint bottle of my favorite bourbon. That bottle was still almost half-full when the summer ended, but I did derive some obscure kind of comfort from its presence on the bathroom shelf.

"Again, soon after I had turned out the reading light, the steps came up the stairs, as firmly as before. This time they went along the hall and on up to the top floor, where they stopped. Again I investigated, and again found no trace of anyone. This, I decided, was the moment to sample the bourbon.

"All summer long those steps returned, sometimes once a week, sometimes every night that I was in the house. Many nights I cannot vouch for, because I developed a knack for going quickly to sleep, after closing my bedroom door.

"Once or twice I tried *talking* to the invisible owner of those footsteps, asking what it was all about, and even using the prescribed routine of suggesting that they go away in the name of the Father, the Son and the Holy Ghost. I did learn that turning on the light, or speaking, stopped the steps. If they later recommenced, I was asleep before they did, but *they never came down the stairs.*

"As you see, this is a very simple story of haunting. The best word I can think of for the sensation that it gave me is 'disquieting.' I have had my share of real fright, in and out of wartime, and this was not fright—merely a kind of unpleasant uneasiness.

"When the summer ended and my landlady had returned, I went around to the house with my set of keys.

" 'Thanks,' I said, handing her the keys, 'I understand now why you didn't try to rent the place.'

76

"Her face assumed an expression of relief, gratification and amusement, and I knew that I didn't have to explain further.

" 'Then *you* heard him, too?' she asked.

" 'How could I *help* hearing him?' I countered.

" 'No wonder the house was so cheap,' she continued. 'I have never been able to find out the history of this place, but someone told me that an elderly manservant died here years ago and that his room was on the top floor.'

"Since I never expected to make any use of the story," Mr. Sloane concluded in his letter to me, "the need for the usual 'corroborative witness' didn't occur to me. I do know that my landlady and all four of her children heard the footsteps, and I know also that the house had been sold for much less than its true worth.

"Since that time, the house has changed hands again, and I don't know whether the steps continue or not, since I have never been back in it.

"The haunting seemed like so many others—more dramatic and carefully authenticated stories—that I didn't follow it up, but here it is, for what it is worth, to add to your collection of *true* ghost stories."

BUELL MULLEN'S STORY

Buell Mullen is an internationally famous artist who specializes in a unique and highly skilled occupation, that of etching and painting on stainless steel. Her steel murals, worked out in a huge studio overlooking Central Park South, decorate the Library of Congress in Washington, the General Motors Building in Detroit, the International Telephone and Telegraph Building in Nutley, New Jersey, and public buildings in Brazil and other foreign countries. President Eisenhower's gift to the famous Seventh Regiment on its 150th birthday was a portrait of himself, etched and painted on steel especially for the occasion by Mrs. Mullen.

This talented woman told me of a bizarre experience that happened to her several years ago and to this day leaves her baffled. This was one ghost—or whatever it was—that served a useful purpose, by giving a warning that quite possibly saved a friend's life.

Mrs. Mullen was vacationing in northern Michigan and paying a visit to the summer home of a friend, Celeste McVoy Holden, at Pentwater, on Lake Michigan, north of Grand Rapids. The house was large and rambling, with several wings, and was set back from the road in a somewhat isolated location.

Mrs. Mullen, Mrs. Holden and the latter's four-month-old daughter and her nurse were the only people in the house at the time. The servants and the chauffeur lived in nearby Pentwater, coming in for their daily duties. Mrs. Holden had recently obtained a divorce from her husband—an unfriendly, unpleasant divorce, due to his dour disposition—and she had temporary custody of their baby.

Mrs. Mullen was expecting her husband to join them at Pentwater and, at the time of the unusual occurrence herein detailed, she was sitting in her room, writing him a note

78

outlining the best ways of getting to Pentwater from Chicago. Suddenly, the hand with which she was writing was seized, as if by a cramp, and the words "beware . . . beware" appeared on the paper, in a handwriting not her own. After several wild gyrations of the pen, during which she felt that she had lost control of her hand, the word "Jack" appeared. Then the writing stopped.

Mrs. Mullen was too shaken by this experience to attempt to finish the letter. Instead, she rushed to her friend Celeste and speechlessly handed her the note. Mrs. Holden's face went white. "Jack" was the name of her husband.

"Let's see if we can find a ouija board that will finish the sentence," Mrs. Holden suggested. Mrs. Mullen agreed, and the two of them set off for the village in search of one. In Pentwater they located a toy shop which, surprisingly enough, did have ouija boards for sale. They bought one and returned to the house.

The ouija board, with their four hands touching it, began to operate immediately, and the first words that came through were "murder . . . you and the child . . . beware."

By now thoroughly frightened, Mrs. Holden asked the board, "Shall we call the police?"

"No . . . useless . . . prepare," was the board's response.

"Shall I phone my husband in Chicago?" Mrs. Mullen then asked the board.

"No . . . too late," the board responded, then stopped altogether.

Mrs. Holden knew that her chauffeur, who lived in the village, had a gun. She phoned him and asked if he would be available in case they needed protection. He was baffled by the request, but said that he would be.

The two women then took the nurse and the child to a remote wing of the house, after giving them their supper, and proceeded to barricade all the doors that led to the outside. Then they sat down, fearfully, to await developments.

Neither of them went to bed that night and they kept themselves awake by playing cards. When morning came and nothing had happened they both felt rather foolish, and had a good laugh at themselves.

A couple of days later, Mrs. Holden had a phone call from

her cousin, John Malloy, from nearby Harbor Point. He immediately asked her if she had had a call from her estranged husband, and went on to explain why he was calling:

"We were having a dance up here at Harbor Point night before last," he said, "and Jack came in, roaring drunk and flourishing a gun. Kept saying he was going to kill you, Celeste, and the baby, too. He had passed through Pentwater earlier that evening, so maybe it's just as well that you weren't down in the village, seeing a movie, or something. We managed to keep him out of trouble and he left the Point around three o'clock in the morning."

"That's all there is to the story," Mrs. Mullen concluded. "Celeste never saw her husband again. Sometime later, she learned that he had become a hopeless mental case, which probably explained his ungovernable rages. He died about ten years later."

RUSSELL PATTERSON'S STORY

Ouija boards figure in a great many stories of the super-natural; planchette boards are much rarer. A planchette, in case you don't know, is a small, three-cornered board (the word in French means "little plank") shaped like a ouija board but with this difference: one of the three legs of the little table is a pencil; so, instead of merely pointing at the letters of the alphabet, it actually writes out its messages.

It was a planchette that had a lot to do with dictating his art studies in Paris, Russell Patterson told me, as well as exposing some phony cardsharps who were taking friends of theirs for a beautiful ride.

"I've only met two people who could get any real results with a planchette board, and one of them was my former wife, Constance," said Russell, who for many years has been a highly successful illustrator, poster artist and decorator of swank New York night clubs.

"In my art student days in Chicago, we had known James and Dorothy Dulan. Dorothy, as you know, was fashion artist on your own paper, the New York *Daily News*. Jimmy's claim to fame is that he was author of at least one book that I know of—a book illustrated with etchings by a man named Webb. Jim and Dorothy had been living in Paris for some time and when Constance and I went there, we looked them up. It was Dorothy who introduced us to planchette.

"We were invited to their house one night for a sort of 'planchette party.' Jim and Dorothy could get some results with the board, but for them it operated quite slowly.

"One of the guests that night was William Burton, who was studying portraiture in Paris. Bill was heir to the Bernheimer fortune and had a large income, which he spent quite freely. You may remember, his name was much in the news a few years ago when his daughter Patricia (Patsy) was

81

murdered by her husband, Wayne Lonergan, in New York. Bill had, of course, died long before that.

"Bill Burton apparently went on the theory that money could buy anything. That night he said he would pay just about anything to learn to operate a planchette board. He tried it with one after another of the guests at the party, but nothing happened. Finally, he asked my wife Connie if she wouldn't try to work it. He said if she would only make the effort, just put her hands on the board, he would give a big party for everybody present. Connie did put her hands on the board with Bill and it started working immediately— writing clearly and rapidly.

"At the time, Bill was living in a large old house in Paris of which he occupied only two floors, one as a studio. He had rented the house from a couple, a man and his wife, about whom he knew little or nothing, and he certainly knew nothing about the background of the house.

"The first message that came from the planchette board purported to come from the mother of his landlady. The 'spirit' said she was a countess and formerly owned the place. Toward the end of her life, she said, both her daughter and son-in-law had made her very unhappy. They had locked up all her pictures, papers and personal belongings in a small room on the third floor, next to the bedroom that she had occupied. As proof that she was telling the truth, she said there was a small picture hanging near her bed that had been autographed by the Pope.

"Bill investigated and, sure enough, found the bedroom as the 'countess' had described it. And, hanging by the bed *was* the picture with the Pope's autograph! And next to the bedroom there was another bedroom, apparently the 'small room' described, that was securely locked!

"Well, after that, Bill could hardly stay away from the planchette board, and he ran Connie ragged asking her to demonstrate it for his friends.

"Both Bill and his wife were avid bridge players and they had guests in two or three nights every week to play. Bill almost always lost, and it was costing him around five hundred dollars a week.

"Among their guests were a man and his wife—I presume she was his wife—who played bridge every night, somewhere, and they were consistent winners. The planchette board, with Connie and Bill working it, warned him against this couple. The 'countess' said they were cheating and that if we would follow instructions and watch them carefully we would learn how. The message was, 'Watch the necklace.'

"The next time they played at Bill's studio, all of us— Connie, myself and Bill's wife, that is—kept a close watch. The woman had a rather flashy necklace, which she was constantly fingering, as if to see that it were still there (you've seen women do this, of course). But she wasn't just fingering her necklace idly. By checking back and comparing notes, we learned that she actually was giving signals to her husband, and it didn't take us long to break the 'code.' As a result of this, we did a bit of investigating and learned that they weren't just 'rich Americans,' in Paris for fun as they pretended to be, but a couple of cardsharps who played the social game and lived quite well on their earnings.

"Bill Burton became such an addict of the planchette board that he followed us around everywhere, and when Connie and I came to New York he followed us there and even took an apartment across the street.

"However, to get back to what the planchette board did for me . . . For some unknown reason, I could only get messages at one o'clock in the morning—with Connie acting as the 'control,' naturally. The first message I got in a series of art discussions told me that my painting was too cold; said I should get a warmer glow and suggested that I could get it by adding sepia to my palette. On one occasion, it gave me a quite scholarly criticism of something I was working on. Connie didn't know what I was painting at the time, and in any case, she wouldn't have been able to give a technical criticism.

"The handwriting was particularly beautiful, and the messages well expressed. Once, the messages purported to come from Leonardo da Vinci! I knew practically nothing about da Vinci's work and on the planchette board's advice I went to the Louvre to make a study of his paintings. And I did observe the brilliancy and 'gold light' in his paintings that the planchette board had described.

"The planchette told us to get *The Works and Memoirs of Leonardo da Vinci*—I am not sure now if that was the exact title, but at any rate it was something quite similar— and observe, on a certain page (giving the page number), how very *modern* he was. We couldn't locate a copy of this book in Paris but later, when we went to England, we found

83

one in London. On the page mentioned was the story of how da Vinci had tried to invent a flying machine! We had a great many messages along this line, and I can truly say that the planchette board's 'criticisms' definitely helped me in my own painting.

"After Connie and I came to live in New York, Wilda Bennett and her husband, Peppy de Albrew, moved in next to us. You'll probably remember Wilda as the star of several musical comedies and one of the most beautiful dancers in New York. She and Peppy were among the most popular dance teams in vaudeville and in the better night clubs. At that particular time, they had just returned from a long stay in Europe and were having a rather hard time getting re-established in New York.

"One night, Wilda came into our apartment when Bill Burton was there, working the planchette board, as usual, with Connie. Wilda asked for a message and got one: she was not to be discouraged, it said, because she and Peppy would shortly have their names 'up in lights' and *in two places*. Soon after that they did get an unexpected call, or rather two calls, and were engaged simultaneously for appearances at the Palace Theatre and the Montmartre, a Broadway night club.

"After that, Wilda, too, became a planchette addict, and she became almost as good at operating the board as Connie —though perhaps Connie was the 'control' all along; I don't know. Anyway, after that, we had Wilda and Peppy around our necks, practically, as well as Bill Burton. Once, when Wilda and Connie were at the board, Wilda got a message advising them to call Marcus de Albrew, Peppy's brother. It said he was in a dangerous way 'mentally.' They put a phone call through to Marcus and asked him to come right over. He did; and when they told him why they had called, he admitted that he had been in a very low state and, in fact, was contemplating going up on the roof and jumping off when the phone rang!

"Our apartment became so popular that we finally stopped answering the doorbell or the phone because it was usually some of the friends of Wilda and Peppy, come to get messages from the planchette. The whole business was making Connie sick and nervous, and she decided to give it up for good.

"She did get one final message before she stopped it alto-

84

gether. On the night the news broke of the Lindbergh kidnaping, she decided to try and see if she could get some
message by working the planchette. The board answered
her question, all right: its message, in these exact words,
were, 'There is no use trying. The child is out of this
world.'"

JEANNE OWEN'S STORY

To Jeanne Owen, head of the New York Chapter of the Wine and Food Society, I am indebted for a story about one of the meanest ghosts who ever lived—the ghost of a man who hated his wife and his children, and the house they built to get away from him. He probably hated himself most of all, and it would have served him right if he went up in smoke, along with the home he helped to destroy.

Mrs. Owen's encounter with him is still so vivid in her mind that she recalls the sound of his footsteps on the gravel drive outside her window, and how badly he frightened her dog. And she is so insistent on getting the details correct that her story is accompanied with a graphic, and apparently accurate, map of the locale where it took place— drawn by herself.

"I know it is the thing to call anything resembling a farm a *ranch* in California, but in this case it was a farm—Spring Hill Farm—tucked away on a back road in the hills of Napa Valley, about four miles from the drowsy little town of St. Helena. Three miles off the main road, reached by a bumpy dirt road, and glimpsed through an opening in the overlapping hills, it came into view.

"Originally, it was a plain country house, without benefit of any architectural skill, surrounded by a broken-down fence and weed-choked orchards, plus a few dusty olive trees that struggled to give some shade from the hot California sun.

"Back of the house, up on the hill, was another building: a small, two-room shack that wasn't fit for man or beast. It had a door and two windows, facing *into* the hillside, with its back to the lovely view of the valley. This shabby cabin seemed to have no excuse for existence; not as a refuge for farm animals and certainly much less as a habitable dwelling for humans. One reached it by following a narrow path up the hill.

"This farm was the property my son chose to 'fix up' after he left college and married Dorothy, a pretty Irish girl from the big city, meaning San Francisco. My son, George, had completed an expensive education at the University of California Agricultural College and intended to develop the place and put it on a paying basis as a modern ranch.

"Following his own plans, he started remodeling the house, and a very pleasant place it was when ready for occupancy by a family of three, the baby meanwhile having arrived. The rebuilt dwelling was patterned after the modern California ranch house style, with a guest bedroom in the front, looking onto a narrow porch, facing the drive.

"This drive had been gravelled by my son to offset the damage by rains, which drained down the hill and reduced the road to a sea of mud in winter. It led from the gate to the front door, ending in a circle which was a dead end; one could go no farther.

"This gravel drive had the equal advantage of alerting the approach of cars, pedestrians, or unwanted cows that might wander in from the pasture. It is important that you get this picture in mind.

"My visits from New York to California were spent at Spring Hill Farm, with periodic trips to San Francisco— now don't laugh—to catch up on sleep! For the guest room at my son's house, which they called 'Jeanne's Room,' wasn't conducive to restful slumber. Every night, specifically between the hours of midnight and 2:00 A.M., I was disturbed by the sound of footsteps on the gravel drive. Who could it be, and why should *anyone* be strolling abroad at this hour? Every time it happened, I would leap from my bed and rush to the window, but I never saw anything until one moonlit night . . .

"My son owned a large and beautiful German police dog that always slept on the front porch outside my window, and it was the behavior of Nick, as they called him, that bothered me most of all.

"Nick was an excellent and protective watch dog, and I felt sure he would never permit anything *living* to approach the house. The sound of the footsteps on the gravel always

87

awakened him, too. He would start growling; then he would jump off the porch and start in pursuit of some invisible object, only to return, whimpering, as if he had been struck!

"On that particular moonlit night, I *did* see something, though it was only a shadow—the shadow of a man, apparently. It moved to the end of the gravel drive and disappeared around the corner of the house, beyond which was the narrow path that led to the shack on the hill!

"Nick saw it also and started in pursuit. But a few seconds later he was back, crouching on the floor and whimpering, as if he were in pain.

"I spoke of this unexplainable thing several times to my son, but I always got the same reaction: 'Oh, Mother!' in that slightly patronizing tone that the younger generation employs when brushing off the foolish fancies of their elders.

"However, I had a friend at court, so to speak: the brother-in-law of my son's wife, Dorothy, a doctor by profession and a charming gentleman. On one of my trips to San Francisco, I took Dorothy along, for a change of tempo and a bit of shopping. The doctor took us out for dinner at one of San Francisco's many fine restaurants, and the story came out.

"It seems that he had spent a month at Spring Hill Farm, convalescing from an illness, just before I had arrived for *my* first visit. He enlarged on the charm and beauty of the location; on what my son had done to improve the property, et cetera, then added: 'There is only one disadvantage; I can't sleep when I am there.'

"I waited for him to continue before describing my own experiences.

" 'I would give anything to know who it is that walks on the gravel drive in front of the house every night, between twelve and two, then disappears to nowhere. It bothered the dog, too.'

"Dorothy looked at me with a frightened stare. I smiled and remarked, a little smugly, 'Apparently I'm in my right mind, after all.'

"Dr. Hill and I then discussed the mystery at length, compared notes, and learned that our experiences were identical. We both decided that Dorothy should, if possible, find out what had happened at Spring Hill in the past.

"I had returned to New York and the midnight disturbances at Spring Hill Farm had just about passed out of my mind when I received a letter from Dorothy which brought it all back. Here is the part of her letter that concerns my story:

" 'I had put the baby to bed and George and I were having dinner on the summer dining porch, which, as you know, opens from the center of the living room. George was facing the room, his back to the garden. He was talking to me about something—I don't remember what—when he suddenly stopped, in the middle of a sentence. I looked up and saw that he was staring directly past me at something in the room. His expression frightened me, so I turned around quickly, to see what it was that had startled him so. And I was absolutely petrified by what I saw. A tall, gaunt old man, smoking a cigarette, was walking out of the back hall and across the room, going toward the front door. I jumped up and rushed into the bedroom, to see if the baby was all right. He was sleeping peacefully. As I went back to the table, I could smell stale cigarette smoke, but our visitor was nowhere to be seen. George searched the place and also went outside, but there wasn't a trace of him.

" 'I shall go to see Mrs. Irwin tomorrow. (Dorothy's letter continued.) She is eighty-five years old, or more, and knows the history of every family and every place for miles around.'

"Dorothy's next letter described her visit with the old lady. Yes, Mrs. Irwin said she knew the background of Spring Hill Farm very well, and said she had wondered why any young couple would want to live there. School children called it 'the haunted place,' and always started running when they passed the gate.

"For many years, it seemed, the only house on the place had been the small two-room shack on the hill. It had been occupied by a couple, a very strange man and his wife, who

89

was a good farm woman. She bore him three sons and the family of five continued to live in that miserable shack until the boys were almost grown. It seemed impossible that five human beings could live so long in such quarters, but Mrs. Irwin said they did—cooking, sleeping and eating in those two small rooms, without running water or conveniences of any kind. The meanness and tyranny of the father had become a subject for neighborhood gossip for miles around.

"The boys kept promising their mother that when they were old enough, they would build her a real home. They eventually did, and it was the house that they constructed themselves, on the lower slope, that my son bought. When the boys were building it, the old man swore that they would never live in it—he would see to that. But the boys went ahead in spite of him.

"When the house was completed sufficiently to move in, the man threatened to kill his wife if she left him to go live in it. The neighbors remembered that he would break into violent fits of rage, and that his anger was simply inconceivable. So, one day, the boys took their mother away. No one ever knew where they went; they just quietly disappeared from the neighborhood.

"The old man went on living in the two-room shack, bitter, alone, and speaking to no one. The vineyardist farther up the mountainside for a long time had been delivering demijohns of homemade wine to him; just leaving the demijohns at the gate, full, and taking away the empty demijohns that were left outside at night by the old man, who didn't want to see or talk to anyone.

"One day, school children passing the gate noticed that a full demijohn of wine was still in the yard, where it had apparently been left several days before. The next day it was still there, and the next. So the children reported this to their parents, who in turn reported it to the authorities in St. Helena.

"Several men from the village then came up to investigate. They found the door to the shack bolted from the inside, so they broke a window and got in that way. Inside, lying on a filthy, unmade bed, was the old man—dead. The body was removed and given burial in a local potter's field.

"This might have been the end of the old man," Mrs. Owen went on, "but apparently it wasn't. The place remained unoccupied, with no one to claim it, until my son took possession. Unoccupied, that is, unless you can believe that the spirit of that evil old man was still hovering around, more angry than ever, now that a happy family was living in the house that his sons had built for their mother—angry, and just waiting to cause trouble for whoever lived in it.

"The next time I heard from Dorothy there had been a real tragedy for them: the complete destruction of their home! My son had been called to San Francisco on business and was obliged to leave Dorothy there, alone, with the baby. With the German police dog for protection, she had no fear. Dorothy had retired for the night and was in bed, reading, when she smelled smoke. It seemed to come from the back of the house, and she got up to investigate. To her astonishment and horror, she discovered the entire back porch and kitchen were in flames!

"Dorothy rushed back into the bedroom, snatched up the baby, and ran into the living room to the telephone. She called the St. Helena operator and asked her to alert the local fire department. She had only time to wrap herself and the baby in blankets and get out of the house before the entire place was blazing.

"The whole village of St. Helena turned out, but by the time help arrived, it was too late. The firemen found Dorothy sitting on the front lawn, with only a blanket over her nightgown, watching everything they possessed going up in smoke.

"When my son returned from San Francisco, he was confronted by the charred ruins of what had been his home. All that was left was the concrete wall and the cement cellar floor that had been part of the original house.

"My son didn't rebuild immediately, and when he did, he built *around* this floor, making a patio of the cellar space. It may seem like superstition, but, frankly, I think he was wise in doing so. George had come to the conclusion that what the ghost of that old mountain man hated was the house his sons had built for their mother—and he wasn't taking any further chances.

"The new house that he built is a beautiful, modern ranch house that includes a guest room for me. I have been back to visit Spring Hill Farm many times since, and in the new

91

home I haven't been troubled by sleepless nights. The ghost of the old mountain man apparently has gone to rest; perhaps he went up in smoke in the fire that he obviously helped to start."

BURL IVES' STORY

Burl Ives, the troubador who turned actor and electrified Broadway with his first big dramatic performance in *Cat on a Hot Tin Roof*, is of Scottish-Irish descent, and therefore might be expected to have had a few brushes with the supernatural. As I discovered, he has had quite a few, a couple of which he has given me permission to add to this collection.

"While driving to a house about an hour's ride from Dublin," as Burl tells it, "I was occupying the back seat of a small car. A woman friend was driving and another woman occupied the front seat alongside of her. We were heading for the home of a mutual friend, with whom we were all to dine.

"About twenty minutes before we reached the house of our hostess, I noticed a figure standing in the road, directly in our path. It was approaching dusk, but even in that dim light I could tell that the figure was that of a man, wearing a large cloak.

"Like most back-seat drivers, I was tempted to cry out and warn the driver, but just before we reached the spot where the man had been standing, he disappeared. My impression was that he had paused only momentarily in the middle of the road, then had crossed over it, to the side that was bordered by a low stone wall. Beyond this wall was a sheer drop, which would have made an exit by this route very dangerous, unless a person were extremely sure-footed. At the time, it occurred to me that whoever the person was, he was taking quite a chance to attempt to climb down that bank.

"After we passed the spot, I mentioned this to the two women in the front seat, and then learned that *neither of them had seen the man.* This, of course, aroused my curiosity, and when we arrived at our destination, I mentioned

93

the incident to my hostess. She smilingly explained that many people coming down that road had seen the man—or a man—at just that spot. On the other hand, just as many hadn't! In short, he was an apparition.

" 'Do you know who he is—or was?' I asked.

" 'Yes,' she answered. 'Or, at least, I know who he is supposed to have been. It is one of the local legends that St. Kevin sought refuge from the world in a cave near here. A woman found her way to his hiding place and succeeded in making the holy man break his vows and make love to her. St. Kevin was so overcome with remorse—the story goes —that he killed the woman, and then did away with himself by leaping over the stone parapet that borders the road, at the spot where you say you saw the apparition disappear.'

"I had another rather odd experience while traveling through Scotland," Burl continued. "It couldn't be called a 'ghost story' but it does have an element of the supernatural.

"It was in what they call the 'Rob Roy country,' where the grave of the Scottish hero is located. I had expressed a wish to see his grave, which is up in the hills, and was being taken there by a local guide.

"I had never been in this part of the country before, and had never had this particular trip described to me by anyone. Yet as we progressed I began to describe quite accurately just what we could expect to find on the path that lay ahead of us. At one point, I remember, I stopped, closed my eyes and said: 'In about five minutes we are coming to a bend in the path. Just around that corner are three giant boulders.' Then I went on to describe them further.

"The boulders were there, all right, when we reached that spot, and my description had been so accurate that the guide was astonished—but no more astonished than I was.

"As I said, I had never made the trip before, but doubtless many of my forebears had. So it can probably be put down to race memory. Rob Roy was one of my Scottish ancestors."

Dining with Burl Ives that evening, in his New York apartment, was a friend, a Mrs. Donaldson, a native of Manhattan but now living in the Midwest.

When Burl had finished his story, Mrs. Donaldson smiled

and said "I think I have a story that will interest you." She then told me the story, which follows, about a dream that had particular significance. I asked for her permission to use it. She not only assented, but when she returned home to Indiana, wrote out the story in all its strange and fascinating details. She asked only that I not identify the people concerned too closely, since it would bring up such tragic memories for all of them.

ELLA DONALDSON'S STORY

Ella Donaldson (Mrs. H. M. Donaldson) has for the past fifteen years been employed as an editor by book publishers in both New York and Chicago, and also by a university press. During the war, she edited technical publications for the Army and Navy, in Washington.

Some people dream in symbols and some people dream "true," and Mrs. Donaldson's story concerns a case of dreaming true, even to hearing words—the identical words —spoken in a dream that she was to hear again, in real life.

"I should have preceded my story with a slight prologue," Mrs. Donaldson added, in her letter. "Before the incident I described happened, I did have some prescience of what was to come—a sort of warning, you might call it.

"It was while my friend, whom we'll call 'Patricia,' and I were visiting together in the South. We were sharing an attractive little guest cottage on the estate of some friends of hers. Like so many houses in that particular Gulf state, there was no central heating arrangement, and the house, which was set on the edge of a rather damp garden, was provided only with an open gas heater. This was for use in case the nights got cool, which they certainly did. The spring weather that year was interrupted by a severe cold spell, and the gas heater was very welcome.

"Patricia's customary way of insuring warmth enough was to light the gas heater at bedtime and shut the doors and windows, until morning. I told her that this was exceedingly dangerous; in fact, I was pretty cross about it, and was so insistent about the danger that Patricia finally gave in and consented to keep at least one of the windows partly open.

"About six months after this incident, Patricia wrote me from New York stating that she had become engaged to a friend of long standing, Henry (which isn't his real name),

96

and invited me to visit her in New York before taking off. I was to stay at her sister's apartment and share the guest room with her (Patricia).

"When I got to New York, Patricia explained that Henry now had an excellent position overseas, and since she intended to live abroad after their marriage, she thought it best to marry him over there and save his 'leave' for a real visit home, in perhaps a couple of years.

"The guest room had twin beds, one for each of us. The next morning after my arrival I woke up to find the twin bed occupied by someone else. Instead of Patricia, with her long, fair hair and her usual expression of cheerful repose, there was a much older woman, with *bushy gray hair*. The woman resembled Patricia's mother, but seemed much older, and had a tired, tragic expression on her face.

"As I continued to gaze at her, this person awoke and sat up. Turning toward me, she remarked, with infinite sadness, 'I wonder where Patricia is now.'

"A sudden, cold fear took hold of me.

" 'Where *could* she be?' I asked, almost in a whisper.

" '*In a coffin, on the high seas,*' the woman answered mournfully.

"With a shudder, I woke up, and found it had all been a frightful dream. The morning was bright and sunny, and there, sleeping peacefully in the twin bed, was Patricia.

"A few minutes later she awoke.

" 'Do you suppose we could sleep a little longer?' she asked, drowsily. 'Or do you want your coffee now?'

"I replied that it was still early, and suggested that she sleep a while longer; that I would go and get some coffee.

"In the dining room, I found three members of the family were already up and having breakfast. Without mentioning my disturbing dream, and the premonition of evil that I still hadn't shaken off, I ventured my opinion that Patricia might be making a mistake by going overseas now, and asked what chances there were of dissuading her.

" 'Absolutely none!' replied one of the family. 'None of us approved of the idea from the first. But she is bound and determined to go through with it and I don't think you or anyone else can succeed in changing her mind.'

"Shortly after this, Patricia joined us in the dining room, looking her usual cheery self. Because of my dream, I decided I *would* try to change her mind.

97

" 'I had a bad dream last night . . .' I began.

" 'You look it!' Patricia interrupted. 'But you can have a nice nap this afternoon and catch up on sleep. This is our day to go shopping.'

"So I never mentioned my dream, to her or anyone else.

"The plans went ahead for the wedding. Finally Patricia, very chic in a new traveling outfit and looking radiantly happy, took off by overseas plane, and we all saw her off at the airport.

"The next day the family received a cable saying she had 'arrived safely.' A few days later, allowing for time for an air-mail letter to reach the States from abroad, was a note from Patricia—still radiantly happy. The marriage had gone through per schedule and Henry already had a small furnished flat, where they could start housekeeping immediately.

"On the heels of this letter—if I remember rightly, almost on the day of its receipt—came another cable, from some civil authority, stating that Patricia and Henry were *dead!* Details were to follow.

"The following days for us in New York passed in a blur of shock and grief. We struggled with overseas phone calls, cables, correspondence, then finally pieced together the tragic story.

"Patricia and Henry had died of asphyxiation; killed by monoxide poisoning from a defective *gas heater* in the living room of the little apartment that Henry had rented. The janitor of the apartment house had found them together, dead, in the living room; all windows shut and the gas heater still burning. He told the investigators that the lady had complained of feeling cold the day before. He stated that the heater had been used before and hadn't been defective, so far as he knew.

"Then came further word that the required formalities had been completed by officials of the local government, by our own consul, and by representatives of Henry's company. Per instructions from Patricia's family, her body would be shipped back to New York in a sealed coffin, and the name of the ship and the date of sailing were given.

"Patricia's mother, who had come on to New York, had taken the shock of her daughter's death with extraordinary fortitude. Oddly enough, one of the things that seemed to upset her most was news that a dreadful storm on the At-

lantic was delaying the arrival of passenger ships from overseas. One of the ships being held up by the storm was the
liner carrying Patricia's body.

" 'If only she could have had a smooth crossing,' she
sighed.

"On her arrival, Patricia's mother was placed in the guest
room with me, in her daughter's New York apartment—
occupying the same twin bed in which Patricia had slept.
The next morning, I awoke and found her still sleeping.
Her face, looking very tired and tragically changed by the
shock of Patricia's death, was framed by a mass of *bushy
gray hair!* I had always seen her wearing it neatly brushed
back, in a tight knot at the back. I was immediately re-
minded of the woman I had seen in that horrid nightmare.

"As I continued to stare at her, she awoke and sat up.

" 'I wonder where Patricia is now,' she murmured, with
infinite sadness.

"The exact words the woman with the bushy hair had
used in my dream!

" 'Where *could* she be?' I manage to whisper. The next
few seconds were almost unbearable, because I knew exactly
what she was going to say before she said it:

" *'In a coffin, on the high seas,'* was her sorrowful reply."

MAE WEST'S STORY

About the last person you would suspect of having an interest in psychic phenomena is that spectacular and very tangible personality, Mae West. But Miss West *is* deeply interested in spiritualism and makes no bones about it. Far from being evasive in discussing such things, she is eager to spread the word—to the right people—about something that has answered a spiritual need for her and given her a deep inner satisfaction.

I had gone backstage to interview Miss West at the Latin Quarter night club on Broadway, where she was playing to packed houses in a highly amusing and slightly ribald act involving eight young athletes whom she called her "muscle men."

In the course of our conversation, I asked her if it was true that Mr. Ralph Pressing (mentioned elsewhere in this book) had given her a demonstration of trumpet mediumship, as he claimed. She nodded assent.

"Then you *are* interested in spiritualism?" I inquired.

"Definitely," Miss West replied.

Sensing a story, I asked: "How did it come about?"

"I first became interested in spiritualism several years ago, when I was at the peak of my success as a movie star in Hollywood," Miss West answered.

"This may seem an odd way of putting it, but I was satiated with success. I didn't become interested in psychic phenomena because of any personal tragedy; it was from a completely different angle.

"I had proved my ability as a playwright on Broadway, after a long and successful career as an actress, and had made a great name for myself—as well as a great deal of money—as a movie star. I had acquired most of the things that usually satisfy a woman's desires, but it wasn't enough.

" 'What,' I kept asking myself, 'is beyond all this? Is

100

there a *hereafter*, and what proof do we have that there is?'
I felt that religion could possibly give the answer, and I did
discuss these things, many times, with preachers, priests
and rabbis. Perhaps they themselves were too highly developed to get their ideas across to a mere beginner, but
somehow I derived little satisfaction from what I was told.

"The possibility of life after death continued to fascinate
me. When I read in the Los Angeles papers that there was
to be some sort of spiritualistic convention there, to which
the public would be welcome, I determined to investigate.

"I couldn't very well attend one of these meetings personally, without causing a lot of talk, so I asked my manager
and long-time friend, Jim Timoney, to do so. Jim consented
to go to one of the meetings and bring back a first-hand
opinion on whether he felt it was the real thing, or just a lot
of phony showmanship.

"Jim did attend, and he took along with him one of his
prize-fighter protégés, a young man whom we knew only as
Mickey. Like so many boys who grow up in that atmosphere, Mickey was a sort of 'dese, dem, dose guy'; a dia-
mond in the rough, with very little education or cultural
background.

"Presiding over that particular session of spiritualism was
a man from Buffalo, the so-called 'Reverend' Jack Kelly.
At one point in the proceedings, Mr. Kelly looked in the
direction of Jim and Mickey, who were sitting in the second
row, and said, 'I get the name of S.,' and he rattled off a long
and practically unpronounceable name that might have
been Russian or Polish. Mickey turned to Jim Timoney and
whispered 'That's *my* family name!' Jim was completely
surprised, because he had always thought Mickey was of
Irish descent. They were both in for further surprises.

" 'The father of this man S. is here, with a message for
his son. He wants his son to know that he was killed—murdered—and his body thrown into the water *afterward*.'
(Mickey told Jim later that his father's death had always
been ascribed to drowning.)

"Jim and Mickey were both so impressed with what went
on at that meeting that I decided to learn something about

spiritualism for myself, first-hand. I asked Jim if he could arrange a private sitting for me with Jack Kelly.

" 'If he's that good,' I said to myself, 'I'll share him with others.' So I invited a dozen or so friends and relatives, including my sister, Beverly West, and we had a meeting—I suppose you might call it a séance—exclusively for us. Lest he be suspected of trickery in singling out the persons for whom messages might be intended, Mr. Kelly asked that he be tied to a chair and completely blindfolded.

"Some of the things he told us at that meeting were absolutely astounding—things about which he could not possibly know in advance, and some of which would be decidedly embarrassing to certain people if made public.

"The most interesting and significant revelations that evening, however, weren't along personal lines. They were Jack Kelly's answers to some questions I wrote and placed in a sealed envelope. This took place, I forgot to mention, in the fall of 1941, when war clouds were beginning to hover over our country and everyone was curious about how we might become involved.

"To my first question, 'Will we be in the war?' Kelly's answer was, 'We will have a surprise attack in Hawaii within three months.'

"To question number two, 'How long will the war last?' the answer was 'From five to six years.' To this answer was added something I hadn't asked about, namely, '. . . and President Roosevelt will not live out his *fourth* term.'

"My third question was, 'Will we win the war if we *do* get into it?' Kelly answered, 'Yes. America and England together will win the war.'

"There were many other questions and answers—these along distinctly personal lines—that convinced me that whatever the 'Reverend' Kelly's power was, it was real.

"Sometime after this, my sister Beverly was visited at her ranch in the San Fernando Valley by a man from Brooklyn who had known both of our parents back East. Something Beverly didn't know, of course, was that this man—Berkman, we'll call him—was at that very moment wanted in the East, under suspicion of having done away with his wife. There were newspaper mentions of it and stories on the radio, but Beverly learned nothing about it— for the very good reason that while Berkman was at the ranch, he had contrived to keep the papers out of her sight,

102

and had also managed to keep the radio turned off. Beverly told us later that he had been a very agreeable house guest, making himself useful around the place, et cetera.

"The Los Angeles police learned of this man's whereabouts and came to see me, asking me to co-operate with them in getting him into custody. I went with them to the ranch to question Beverly. She could only tell them that he had left a day or so before, leaving no forwarding address. They were stumped. Since there was nothing else to go on, I decided to call on the services of Jack Kelly.

"I put in a phone call to him at Buffalo, where he lives, and got through almost immediately. I started to tell him the whole story of Berkman, and how we—my sister and I—happened to be mixed up in the case. He interrupted me to say 'The man they're looking for was arrested *twenty minutes ago.*'

"I told this to the detectives. It certainly seemed a slim clue to go on, but they didn't scoff at the idea. Instead, they immediately phoned Los Angeles headquarters and asked if there had been any news of Berkman. And the answer was 'He was arrested in San Diego *half an hour ago!*'

"I learned later that quite a few crimes have been cleared up with the aid of mind readers or psychics.

"Having become interested in spiritualism as an observer, I decided to delve into it deeper. I made the acquaintance of a well-known practitioner, a woman, in Los Angeles, and asked her how to go about developing such powers. I offered her whatever sum of money she might ask for giving this instruction. Her answer was that money couldn't buy such knowledge; it had to be attained only by meditation and serious study.

"She taught me, first, how to go 'into the silence'; how to blank my consciousness and let the inner voice come through. I then became aware that, to some extent, I had been doing this all my life. I remember once sitting at a prize fight and having the entire plot of a play come to me, out of nowhere.

"It is that 'inner voice' that tells us what to do at times when outside aid or advice can be of little or no help. The discovery has given me tremendous confidence and a wonderful sense of peace. It may not be the answer to the life-after-death problem that I was once seeking but it is, in itself, enough. I suggest you try it.

"I could tell you many more interesting things, and some rather amusing ones, that came about as a result of that first meeting in Los Angeles that Jim Timoney and his protégé, Mickey (of course that isn't his real name) attended. Jim, my good friend—a good man, and a good Catholic too—passed on some time ago. And I have an inner conviction that some day he may try to contact me, from the other side.

"Jim's protégé, Mickey, now has his own stable of fighters. Incidentally, Mickey learned later that what Jack Kelly had told him at that first meeting—about his father's death—was correct. And Mickey has developed into quite a successful medium himself. He gets messages by 'spirit writing,' in languages that he doesn't understand, spelled out in words for which he has to go to the dictionary to learn the meaning!"

PAUL COATES' STORY

Paul Coates, a columnist on the Los Angeles *Star-Times*, who also now conducts a highly successful filmed television series called "Confidential File," told me that he was, and still is, frankly skeptical about most psychic phenomena, but admits that in his one attempt to expose a medium's efforts as phony, he came off second-best.

"It is a matter of record that every year in the United States millions of dollars are extracted from people who can't afford it by phony spirit mediums. I'm afraid that we in Los Angeles pick up a good deal more than our share of this tab.

"The fortuneteller racket got so bad here, in fact, that we had to pass a law forcing them out of the city. Many of them moved to the country, just outside the city limits. Many others blossomed out as pious—and prosperous—'churchmen,' preaching some sort of doctrine of spiritualism, which is protected under our Constitutional guarantee of religious freedom. If these so-called preachers also carry on with their old practice of holding private séances, there isn't much the authorities can do about it, since it comes under the head of 'religious counsel' and is paid for by 'love offerings.'

"It was sometime in April of 1954 that 'Confidential File' began an investigation on the subject of spirit mediums, and the first thing we decided to expose, if it should turn out to be phony, was the practice of 'table tipping,' by which some mediums are presumed to get messages from the astral world, to questions popped by their clients.

"We discovered incidentally (and you may take this as a parenthetical aside) that the knowledge that many spiritualists and mediums are fakes doesn't explain away certain mysterious phenomena, nor the limited, but wholehearted beliefs, in certain aspects of the supernatural or supernormal by such an eminent man as Aldous Huxley.

105

"Anyway, we contacted a Mrs. Sophie Williams, who was at that time living in the home of Aldous Huxley. Mrs. Williams is a well-known spirit medium, acknowledged to be one of the best in the country, as a matter of fact, and she agreed to demonstrate 'table-tipping' for us. She claimed that she had been subjected to many tests at Duke University, which has long been conducting a study of supernormal phenomena.

"The test was to be made at the home of people selected by ourselves.

"Present at the first demonstration were the producer of 'Confidential File,' meaning myself, a dentist who practices in this community, the dentist's wife and Mrs. Williams. We all co-operated in the experiment—all putting our hands on the table, that is—which was conducted in a dimly-lit room. After about twenty minutes, the table began to tip and we got some answers to questions, by the rapping method.

"We still couldn't determine if there had been any trickery, so we asked Mrs. Williams if she would agree to another demonstration, during which we would *photograph* the entire séance, using infra-red film. Mrs. Williams told us that we stood a chance of raising the table *completely off the floor* if we would work in absolute darkness. So we had some infra-red film flown from New York for our second experiment—so far as I know, the first of its kind attempted.

"We held our second séance about a week after the first, and this time in complete darkness, as agreed. This time there were present myself as the producer of "Confidential File," Mrs. Coates, the above-mentioned denist and his wife, three or four other persons whose names and identities escape me at the moment, and the entire shooting crew of our filmed television show.

"For this experiment, we used a heavy oak dining table. One of our cameras, with infra-red film, was located *under* the table. Two others were located *above* the table, on opposite sides. In other words, we had the table completely 'covered.' And the room was actually in total darkness.

"We were successful in getting this table to move rather dramatically. We also experienced considerable rapping and message answers. The test began at 1:00 P.M. and lasted until four-forty that afternoon. I might add that before the tests began, we had carefully inspected the table for any possible fraud.

"When the film was developed, we were unable to find any indication of trickery, or traces of any artificial devices that might have been used by the medium.

"This put us in the embarrassing position of having to present a program that set out to debunk spiritualism and hadn't succeeded! Since I personally have very strong reservations about spiritualism—meaning that I am inclined to disbelieve in it thoroughly—I didn't feel inclined to present this program on television without offering some possible answer to the phenomena we had experienced. We therefore contacted Mrs. Williams again and asked if she would agree to take a lie-detector test. She said that she would.

"The test was to be conducted by Mr. Chris Gugas, poligraph director for a private detective agency in the city of Los Angeles, who is also on the staff of 'Confidential File.' Gugas is frequently employed for criminal cases by the City and County Police Departments in this area and is recognized as one of the leading poligraph experts in the nation. He has worked with practically every large law enforcement agency in the United States and has also been a police consultant to several foreign governments.

"Mr. Gugas' test lasted three and a half hours, and the final series of questions were conducted on the program itself. At the conclusion of this final series, we asked Gugas to tell us what he had concluded from the test. His answer was that Mrs. Williams was *not telling the truth*. He also explained, technically, how the poligraph test indicated this (the details of which, unfortunately, I cannot supply).

"Mr. Gugas' announcement of his conclusions was made on the air, and in the presence of Mrs. Williams. She was, naturally, embarrassed and disturbed.

"The reaction to this particular program was immediate and violent. There were hundreds—perhaps thousands— of letters from viewers who strenuously objected to our method of trying to debunk Mrs. Williams' spiritualistic séances. In justification of it, I had to explain that it was the *only way we could attempt to offset what our film had shown*, namely, that no trickery had been involved.

"The average person always suspects that there is some trick device used in table tipping. But if there had been such

107

trickery during our tests with Mrs. Williams, the cameras would have revealed it. The film which proves this is still in 'Confidential File's' possession.

"I'm afraid that our experiment concluded rather unsatisfactorily—for us, that is. And, I might add, it also concluded our friendship with Mrs. Williams. She isn't 'in' now, when we call."

SOME EARLY AMERICAN SPOOKS

Paul Coates isn't the first newspaperman to attempt to investigate spiritualistic phenomena, with the idea of debunking it, though he unquestionably is the first to use infra-red movie film and television equipment for the purpose.

Back in the 1870's, when spiritualism was still as hot a subject almost as atomic energy is today, the New York *Sun* sent one of its crack reporters, Henry S. Olcott, to Chittenden, Vermont, to give a full report on the activities of the Eddy Brothers. Curious people from all parts of the world were flocking there to witness the manifestations of Horatio and William Eddy, who operated out of the family farmhouse. Visitors who received permission to witness their operations were put up as boarders in the farmhouse itself, where they ate in a community dining room.

Many other investigators concluded that the Eddys were utter charlatans, but they convinced Olcott that their demonstrations were genuine. His voluminous reports, illustrated by a staff artist (this being before the day of the camera) were eventually put between book covers—four hundred pages of fine type. The book, published in 1874, is a real curio and an amusing contribution to Americana.

Between the two of them, working alternately and in "dark" circles and "light" circles, Horatio and William materialized some *four hundred different characters*, ranging from a pipe-smoking Indian squaw to some bizarre Orientals, who sang Persian songs and discoursed in Russian. These latter were for the benefit of Mme. Helena Blavatsky, who had come halfway around the world to see the Eddys at work. Mme. Blavatsky, member of a distinguished Russian family, is credited with being one of the founders of the Theosophical Society, which originated in Adya, Madras, India.

The "circle room" where the Eddys held their meetings,

109

was the top floor of the farmhouse. At one end of it was a platform on which was a two-by-eight cubicle built of solid wood, and with no openings except a window, to the rear, which was kept closed, and an opening toward the audience, which was covered by a shawl when the medium, presumed to be tied hand and foot, sat inside and produced his tricks.

Skeptics insisted that the characters evoked from the "materialization box" were merely impersonations by one of the Eddys while the other was acting as the medium. Be that as it may, one weak angle to Olcott's report is that he doesn't reveal what William was doing while Horatio was acting as medium, and vice versa.

In any case, the boys would have required a variety of clothing almost as extensive as that of the Eaves Costume Company—as well as a stock company of actors to fill them —to have put on the shows they did. Pretty good for a couple of illiterate Vermont farmers!

Much of the phenomena produced at the Chittenden farmhouse, as reported by Olcott, is quite ludicrous, viewed as "spiritualistic phenomena," and a good deal of it could be done just as successfully by night club or vaudeville magicians. If the Eddy boys' familiars were around today, they doubtless would be appearing on television shows. But where the real thing left off and the phony began was as baffling to Mr. Olcott in 1874 as it is to us today, reading about it. Olcott, far from debunking the Eddys, wound up as their most sincere protagonist.

One odd angle to the spiritualistic craze that swept the country, and eventually the world, is that most of it originated in New England or upper New York state. The New York *Daily Graphic* for November 24, 1874, reported an interview between one of its editors and Frederick W. Evans, a chief elder of the Society of Shakers, in which Evans claimed that *eleven years* before the so-called "Rochester rappings" of the Fox sisters, "similar and much more striking phenomena" had occurred in the Shaker settlements. Children were seized with trances, or clairvoyant sleeps, in which they answered questions correctly and displayed the power of seeing objects and persons without the use of the "corporeal eye." Evans claimed that he was the first to define spiritualism as a *science* instead of a *religion*. In his opinion, it should be studied in the same manner as agriculture, chemistry or any other of the physical sciences.

From the time the Fox sisters "discovered" spiritualism in 1847 in the little town of Hydesville, near Rochester, until they publicly recanted forty years later at a mass meeting in New York's Academy of Music, the subject was a matter for intense and worldwide investigation, argument and violent controversy. Newspapers on both sides of the ocean devoted reams of space, usually on the editorial page, to discussions of this remarkable method of communicating with the dead, or what hopefully passed as such.

Horace Greeley, editor of the New York *Herald*, was intensely interested in it and was one of the staunchest defenders of the Fox sisters, all three of them—Leah, Margaretta and Kate—even permitting them to occupy his town house when he was away in the country with his ailing wife. Greeley was one of the few friends left, though a sadly disappointed and disillusioned one, when Margaretta and Kate, both by now hopeless and irresponsible alcoholics, recanted—for pay, as it turned out—and declared that their mysterious rappings were achieved by the trick of cracking their knuckle, knee and toe joints! Without the benefit of concealed loud-speakers, which hadn't then been invented, this is manifestly absurd, but the enemies of spiritualism avidly seized on it to discredit spiritualism.

When Margaretta died, a pitiful victim of drugs and drink, in a furnished room in Brooklyn, the nurse who attended her later stated that all hell broke loose in the house that night, and that the violent rappings which accompanied the medium's death could not have been produced by *anyone's* joints, let alone those of a feeble and dying woman.

In 1947, a century after the original Hydesville manifestations, Mariam Buckner Pond's *Time Is Kind: The Story of the Unfortunate Fox Family* was published (Centennial Press). Mrs. Pond, who had married a grand-nephew of the Fox sisters—grandson of their only brother, David Fox—states that nearly every member of the family, down to the last generation, was possessed of unusual powers of one kind or another which might be described as *supernormal*. David, who laid no claim to psychic power and was as disapproving of his sisters' activities as their father, was possessed of prodigious physical strength. He could lift a full barrel of apples and toss it onto a wagon with ease, for example.

The mysterious powers of the Fox sisters, like those of the Eddy brothers, seem to have been inherited and from the mother's side. One of the Eddys' maternal ancestors had been smuggled out of Salem to avoid being tried as a witch, and there are indications that both families for generations had traced a peculiar line. Which postulates the question: was James I right when he insisted on burning witches to destroy the unhappy breed? In both the Fox and the Eddy families, the psychic power was hit-and-miss. Horatio and William were the only two members of their family to become professional spiritualists, and Margaretta and Kate were those with the outstanding talent in theirs, although their much older sister Leah also had some powers along this line and it was she who exploited them.

John David Fox was a blacksmith who originally came from Rockland County but moved to Hydesville, New York, in 1847. The Foxes had seven children in all. One died in infancy; three were to live long lives as quiet, respected country folk; three were to become famous, or notorious, the world over, and two of the latter to die in poverty and tragedy. Fox at one period in his life took to drink and his wife left him. It was after they had become reconciled that the two girls who were to become so famous were born—Margaretta and Catherine.

After moving to Hydesville, Fox started building a new house for himself and his wife and these two daughters. Before it could be finished, winter set in, so they moved into a cottage on land he had bought. The Foxes didn't know it then, but a previous tenant had moved out of this cottage because of its disturbing and mysterious noises.

Margaret and Catherine, thirteen and eleven years old respectively, occupied the back bedroom and their parents slept in the room on the southeast corner. They had all retired early on the night of March 29th, but before any of them had gone to sleep they were disturbed by a loud rapping in the front bedroom. From then on, first in one part of the house, then another, these sounds continued and later were augmented by more sinister noises—such as what sounded like a dead body being dragged downstairs to the cellar, followed by the manipulation of a shovel.

Mr. and Mrs. Fox, who are described as devout Methodists, were appalled and were for moving out at once. The eleven-year-old Katie was more courageous. She worked out some tapping code of her own and was soon communicating with the spook, or whatever it was, whom she addressed as "Mr. Splitfoot."

Katie purported to learn, through these communications, that Mr. Splitfoot was actually the spirit of one Charles B. Rosna, a peddler who had been murdered in this house by the former occupants, a man and a woman, and buried in the cellar.

The manifestations became increasingly violent, taking place in the daytime as well as at night: doors were slammed, furniture dragged about, beds rocked, the bedclothes yanked off the bed, etc. And the four-year-old murder was re-enacted every night, with the most grisly sound effects!

Mr. Fox, in a futile attempt to "lay" the ghost, started digging in the cellar, but only struck water. The oldest sister, Leah, a music teacher who lived in Rochester, took the two young girls to live with her, but the manifestations continued there, in many ways worse than before. With her music teaching business ruined by the notoriety, Leah decided to exploit the powers of the two younger sisters, and so the cult of spiritualism was born.

One bitterly ironical angle to the story is that a decade after the last of the three Fox sisters had died, the mystery of the cottage at Hydesville got a refresher. On November 23, 1904, the Rochester *Democrat & Chronicle* gave a big play to a story, the headlines of which read:

HUMAN BONES DISCOVERED
Found Under Famous House at Newark (Hydesville)
Spirits Right!
The Find Corroborates an Old Story
Was a Man Murdered?

The latest owner of the by-now famous cottage—oddly enough, his name was William Hyde—discovered that the stones in the cellar had been weakened by rains and given

113

way, revealing a false wall. In the space between this wall and the original wall were a number of bones, apparently bearing out the legend of the murdered peddler.

Later the cottage was moved to Lily Dale, New York, where it became a sort of spiritualistic shrine. And a full century after Mr. Splitfoot first manifested himself to Katie Fox, the rappings are still heard—daily and (I understand) on schedule during the summer months. And the tin trunk that once belonged to Mr. Rosna, or a reasonable facsimile thereof, is also on display there.

Lily Dale itself, now in its seventy-fifth year as the spiritual home of spiritualism (if you'll pardon the pun) is one of the strangest spots in the United States. In the winter months, the permanent residents number fewer than a hundred families, but with the coming of warm weather the population expands to some 1,500 persons—men, women and children—all gathered there for one purpose: to investigate, study or actively practice psychic phenomena of one sort or another, but more specifically in efforts to communicate with the dead.

The village, which is in Chautauqua County, about forty miles southeast of Buffalo, is set in a pleasant valley of vineyards and apple orchards, and the community occupies about half a square mile. There is a modest hotel and some 250 cottages, all owned by the National Spiritualist Association. At the time of the adventure described by Ann Marsters, which follows, it also boasted a publication called the *Psychic Observer*, edited by a man named Ralph Pressing, who was assisted by his wife Juliet.

The *Psychic Observer*, which has since moved its headquarters to Chesterfield, Indiana, is a bi-weekly trade publication, printed on slick paper, created specifically to report the activities of spiritualists the world over, and describes itself as "Spiritualism's Pictorial Journal." It contains well-written, well-edited news stories on kindred subjects, with appropriate illustrations. It also runs professional advertisements for the practitioners of spiritualism in its various forms, some of which read like the patent medicine ads of the 1880's—"Health Your Problem? Financial Difficulties?

God is the Great Healer! New Life! New Health! Money back if you are not satisfied!" et cetera.

Mr. Pressing was described to me as "a large, hearty man with bulging blue eyes, who suggested in appearance a traveling salesman rather than the publisher of a spiritualistic journal." I was later to meet him in person—which brings us up to date, with the story told me by Ann Marsters.

ANN MARSTERS' STORY

"Ghosts in farmhouses, ghosts in penthouses, ghosts in theaters, but surely not ghosts in a city room!" I exclaimed.

Ann Marsters laughed.

"Yes," she answered, "in the city room of a great metropolitan newspaper. A ghost that saved the day for me, though I would prefer to call her a *spirit*; the spirit of a little Indian girl—"

"An Indian guide, yet," I commented facetiously.

Ann became serious.

"Yes, if you like; an Indian guide who made my acquaintance, so to speak, at Lily Dale, New York.

"War, as you know, always excites interest in life-after-death stories," Miss Marsters went on, "and in the summer of 1942 my newspaper—Hearst's *Chicago-American*—decided to send me to Lily Dale to do a series of articles on the place.

"My editors knew that I, a veteran newspaperwoman, would not incline to gullibility. I have dealt with too many press agents, too many self-promoters, and various types of charlatans and phonies to be taken in. Incidentally, before being transferred to Chicago, I was a sports writer on Hearst's *Boston American*.

"I went to Lily Dale with an open mind—not to write an exposé but to give an honest account of what I saw and heard. And I took along a staff photographer to make a pictorial record of my experiences.

"Mr. Pressing, the publisher of the *Psychic Observer*, and all those professionally concerned with Lily Dale, were most co-operative, and I must say that they put on quite a show for me.

"I was given entree to the daily classes in 'spiritual healing and philosophy,' to which the faithful were summoned by the ringing of a large bell. There were public and private

116

séances for my benefit; table-rapping sessions and 'materializations' in darkened rooms, where my photographer was permitted to take pictures with the use of infra-red light. One of these, which impressed both of us, showed a trumpet apparently flying over the medium's head. There were even experiments, though not very successful ones, with a 'spirit-controlled' radio.

"Some of the experiments were amusing, some disappointing, and some frankly terrifying—such as disembodied hands tweaking my hair and patting my face during one of the dark-room séances. The spiritualists have an explanation for conducting their experiments in the dark; it seems that all things that are *created*, from the beginning of the world (according to the Bible) to the gestation of a child —or, for that matter, the inception of a new book—are created in darkness. And the mediums regard their line of work as creation.

"There were plenty of phonies among the mediums but it seemed easy to spot them and weed them out. And if the net results were something less than entirely successful—I never at any time felt that the various spirit voices that addressed me belonged to the loved ones from whom they were supposed to come—I felt it was through no lack of sincere efforts on the part of what I might call the 'legitimate' mediums.

"Things happened which I can never hope to understand or explain. I only know that what did occur seemed honest and genuine at the time, and I'll never forget any of it. Neither will my photographer, Ed Miley.

"However, to get back to my story . . .

"Among the 'familiars' that were used by several mediums, but who was the particular 'control' of Ann Taylor— one of Lily Dale's better practitioners—was a youthful spirit called Red Rose. This spirit had previously identified herself with the colony as a young Indian girl who had been burned to death in a prairie fire in some indefinite past. Indians are supposed to be especially successful in acting as go-betweens with the spirit world because of their natural 'earthy' quality.

"Red Rose addressed herself to her audiences, via her chosen medium, in a mixture of pidgin English and modern slang. Judging from her remarks, she was a bit fresh.

"This little Indian spook seemed to take a shine to me.

117

She followed me everywhere—even to my hotel room, apparently. At one séance I was embarrassed as well as astonished when Red Rose gaily sang out, via the unconscious medium, 'You put a safety pin in the lining of your coat. Lazy!' This was a fact: five minutes before taking off for the meeting, I discovered a tear in the lining of my coat. I didn't have time to mend it properly, so I fastened the rent with a safety pin! And there was absolutely no one around to see it—unless it was Red Rose, there in her astral body.

"In the series of seven articles that I wrote about Lily Dale, I didn't mention this incident, as I felt sure my editors wouldn't take it seriously.

"I do my work at home in Chicago and after I had written the first installment of the series for the Sunday paper, I phoned the office for a copy boy. He came to my apartment and I handed him both the original and the dupe, and told him to be sure to deliver it to the Sunday editor *in person*—and, I remember, I even said 'Please!'

"Next day, my editor phoned to remind me that I was getting late with my copy. I was quite astonished, and told him that I had sent the copy to the office the day before, by one of our own copy boys. I even identified the boy.

"Well, he got the kid on the carpet—he was one of our newer copy boys—and while the young man did remember collecting the copy from me and taking it to the office, he had absolutely no recollection of what he had done with it! My editor said he did just about everything short of giving the lad the third degree, but nothing succeeded in jogging his memory of what he had done with the manuscript, which was quite voluminous.

"The Sunday editor said over the phone that I would have to write the article all over again. I protested that I couldn't *possibly* remember all I had written, or just how I had written it, and anyway there was hardly time before the Sunday deadline. The series had been heavily advertised in advance, and the deadline for the Sunday feature section was already at hand. So I went over to the office to see what could be done about it.

"I was standing at the editor's desk, in a state of absolute desperation, when I thought of Red Rose, the friendly little Indian girl-spirit whom I had gotten to 'know' at Lily Dale. If Red Rose could detect a hidden safety pin on the inside lining of my coat, perhaps she could help locate my lost copy!

"Concentrating very hard, I whispered, half-aloud: 'Oh, Red Rose, *please* try to help me!' And, believe me, no one ever uttered a more fervent prayer!

"Almost instantly, I seemed to get an answer.

"With no conscious decision or deliberation on my part —actually, without even a thought of what I was doing—I started walking across the city room, toward a telephone booth that was in the corner. Beside the booth was a small table, on which was piled a number of telephone books. I opened one of them—just which one, I couldn't later remember—and there inside of it was *my copy!*

"Maybe Red Rose knew how it got there; I think she was just as capable of being mischievous as she was of being helpful. But, anyway, that is how she came to my rescue and saved the day—not only for me, but for Hearst's *Chicago-American.*

"I've never had occasion to call on her since, but I have the slightly comfortable feeling that if I ever *do* get myself into another desperate predicament, Red Rose will be my ace-in-the-hole to get me out of it."

I was later to meet Mr. Ralph Pressing in person and I found him just as Ann Marsters had described him: large, jovial, with prominent blue ("pop") eyes and a ruddy complexion. He did, indeed, resemble more a traveling salesman than a man who dealt with psychic phenomena.

Mr. Pressing stated that he had seen something in one of the columns about Greta Garbo becoming interested in psychic phenomena, and asked me for her address (which I, of course, declined to give him) stating that he would like to stage a séance for her sometime.

"We had a demonstration for Mae West," he asserted, grinning broadly, "and had six trumpets floating through the air at once, all giving Miss West messages from the spirit world."

"I come down to New York once a week from Lily Dale to give demonstrations," Mr. Pressing explained. "We hold 'em in some midtown hotel. Just now, I'm using the Taft.

Why don't you come around sometime, on a Thursday night. We'll put on a show for you."

I told Mr. Pressing that I would take a rain check on the invitation. Then I began to look over the copy of the *Psychic Observer* that he had left with me. I found it filled with fascinating articles by an assortment of people, ranging from a story about a Hollywood movie star, complete with "cheesecake" photography, to a by-lined story from a youthful sailor in the United States Navy, who had been raised by his parents in a sort of spiritualist cult and had been conducting séances of his own while on shore leave in Florida.

A few weeks later I, in company with a girl friend, did pay a visit to one of Mr. Pressing's "demonstrations." It was held in a suite at the Taft Hotel and present, besides the medium—a Third Avenue antique dealer who doubled as a professional psychic—were a number of rather well known professional folk: writers, actors and lawyers, several of whom I knew personally.

I had decided, after my first meeting with him, that Mr. Pressing was something of a "name dropper," and it soon became apparent that I was the "name" he was making a play for on this occasion.

To get the medium into the proper mood, the lights were turned off and all those present were requested to sing in unison "Nearer, My God, to Thee." We had barely gotten started when there was a knock on the door. It was the house detective, asking that the party inside desist from singing, or at least do it more quietly. (It is seldom given to us to have an experience that is recognizably unique, but I felt that I was having one then. Certainly few, if any, guests at the Taft Hotel have ever been rebuked, prior to this occasion, for singing "Nearer, My God, to Thee"!)

The medium was seated in the center of the room and shortly after the meeting got under way started emitting noises that sounded like someone with a bad case of laryngitis. The tin trumpet, meanwhile, appeared to be floating about, looking for a receptive listener. Soon it touched me on the knee and I knew that I was being, so to speak, tapped for skull and bones.

"This is your grandfather," came faintly from the trumpet, in a guttural whisper.

"Which grandfather?" I inquired.

"The grandfather on your mother's side," it answered.

Acting on a cue from Mr. Pressing, I then asked the spirit what message it had for me.

"Everything is all right here," it replied—or something equally cryptic and enigmatic.

After a moment of silence, there was a great swooshing in the air, which seemed to be caused by the trumpet as is gyrated rapidly over our heads.

"Sounds like an airplane," one of the guests commented aloud.

"It *is* an airplane," was the trumpet's surprising retort. This was followed by a chuckle, also from the trumpet, and another surprising remark: "I've never been dunked in a lagoon before."

"Is this message also for me?" I inquired.

The answer was "Yes."

"Who is the message from?"

Then, to the audible astonishment of everyone present, the trumpet replied: "Raymond Clapper."

(Raymond Clapper, columnist for the New York *World-Telegram*, was killed—presumably drowned—when the plane he was traveling on as a war correspondent crashed in a lagoon on an island in the South Pacific.)

One of the guests interjected, in a half-whisper: "I thought it might be Ernie Pyle."

The trumpet again chuckled.

"Oh, Ernie Pyle is here too!"

"And what does Mr. Clapper wish to say to me?" I asked.

"You're doing all right," the trumpet answered. "Keep up the good work."

There were other remarks and asides on the part of the trumpet, but this was all that was intended for me.

After the meeting broke up, I invited Mr. Pressing and the medium out for hot cakes at Childs'. I then attempted to get from them some statements that would help me comprehend their philosophy as it applied to the supernatural, but I had no success.

Present at the Taft séance was Ed Bodin, then associated in some managerial capacity with the Bernarr MacFadden enterprises and himself a writer who has turned out quite a lot of material on supernatural subjects. At the time, Bodin asked me if I had been a particular friend of Raymond Clapper. I replied that I not only had not been one of his friends, but that I had never even met or seen him, nor was I even a particularly regular reader of his column. I therefore had no idea of why he should be addressing himself to me—provided it *was* Raymond Clapper—except that I was the only newspaper columnist present at the meeting.

The next morning on my desk at the office was a letter from Bodin, evidently written immediately after the séance and mailed special delivery. In it, he said:

"You may not have known Clapper, but you must have been near his desk, or his bed, or something else that was close to him personally. *That is the way these things work.*"

I started a letter to Bodin, saying that I had never been near *anything* belonging to Raymond Clapper. But I stopped on a half-finished sentence.

I just recalled that the very day before the séance, while driving to my own place in Rockland County, New York, I had passed through the town of Spring Valley. And then I remembered: *this is where Raymond Clapper lived!*

You figure it out.

Mr. Pressing has since moved his lares and penates to Indiana, so isn't around to give further personally-conducted séances in New York. Recently I received in the mail a catalogue of publications put out by his Psychic Observer Book Shop. The publications ranged all the way from a treatise on "Astral Projection" to works purporting to explain how to avoid or cure cancer *by supernatural methods.* There were also ads for "Hard to Get Merchandise," such as aluminum trumpets, ouija and planchette boards, crystal balls, E.S.P. cards, slate-writing equipment and luminous paint!

MRS. ALDEN HATCH'S STORY

"Ghost stories? I'm *loaded* with them! My family, the Gatys, had a long history of extra-sensory perception and practically every one of them—and I've known of four generations—had some experience that might be called supernatural. Shall I tell you about the table that walked upstairs? Or the ghost of the 'McGonigal'? Or the message about 'the dead man down by the creek'? Perhaps I'd better tell you all of them and let you select."

The speaker was the young and pretty wife of biographer Alden Hatch who, under her own name of Allene Gaty, is making quite a reputation as a portrait painter and a cartoonist of wit and perception.

"To understand the supernatural happenings that occurred during my childhood—the walking table was just one of many—perhaps it would be well to describe the house that I was brought up in: the most perfect setting for such happenings that you could dream of.

"The house itself was typical of its Hudson Valley background: a Dutch Colonial brick structure built by Major Dirck Wesselse Ten Broeck. The older wing was built circa 1734. The front and main part had the date of its construction, 1762, marked for posterity with white bricks placed in the façade, spelling out those figures.

"There were heavy shutters that could be closed in time of Indian raids; also portholes up under the eaves from which to take pot shots at marauders. The hand-hewn beams were put together with wooden pegs—an exciting discovery for me as a child.

"Across the creek which bordered our land—a former Indian waterway to the Hudson River—was an Indian burial ground. At the top of the hill was an extensive graveyard containing headstones marking the graves of slaves, indentured servants and members of the Ten Broeck family from 1700 on.

123

"As you can see, there should have been enough spirits to haunt an entire county—spirits of every color, shape and size, all compressed within a three-hundred-foot farm, which seemed to be their favorite stamping ground. I am convinced that the charged atmosphere had a lot to do with the spooky goings-on there.

"Table-tipping became a pastime to while away lonely evenings on a rather isolated farm, and we received many extraordinary 'messages.' My grandmother, whom we nicknamed 'Peter' because she said she would always remain young like Peter Pan (and did), was the best operator, and next to her, oddly enough, were my two young uncles, Jack and Lew Gaty, though they were just out of college and scoffed at the whole idea.

"At the time of the table-walking incident, four aunts and uncles were visitors in the house and Aunt Nan's husband, 'A.B.,' had been teasing his eccentric in-laws about their silly games.

"Peter remarked that the table was 'getting cross,' and that some unfriendly spirit had apparently gotten control. She and Uncle Jack tried to get some sensible messages, but the spirit—or whatever it was controlling the table—became more excited and incoherent. Someone, probably 'A.B.,' facetiously suggested that if the table weren't going to *talk*, perhaps it could *walk*. Whereupon it *did* walk, in a very determined manner, toward the door that led into the central hall.

"Both Peter and Uncle Jack were startled at the table's unexpected behavior, and both had difficulty keeping their fingers touching it as it gathered speed and literally *skipped* out of the room. By this time, all the rest of the family were watching the performance, both amused and astonished at the table's erratic actions.

"When the table reached the hall, it made a sharp right turn angle and started up the staircase. Poor Peter had to back up the stairs and be adroit about it, in order to keep her fingers touching the table as it clattered upward—first one leg, then another—swiftly and with decision. When the table reached the first landing, it turned left and practically *flew* up the remaining stairs, and out of sight of those watching below.

"When the table reached the upper hall it stopped walking and seemed to stamp angrily, twice. Then it stopped moving altogether, and refused to give so much as a quiver the rest of the evening. It acted as though it were exhausted; certainly both Peter and Uncle Jack were.

"Another time, two of my uncles were tipping the table, while my Aunt Helen sat curled up in a window seat, taking down the messages by moonlight. The rest of the room was in darkness and Peter sat in a far corner, quietly knitting.

"Suddenly the table started walking. It crossed the room, straight to Peter's chair—with the manipulators keeping pace with it as best they could—and then started tapping out a message in quick, emphatic raps and with such speed that Aunt Helen could hardly write down the letters, much less make sense of what the table was saying at the time.

"When the table stopped, there was an electrically-charged silence; then everyone rushed simultaneously to turn on the lights. They all felt they knew who the message was from; only one person could fill a room with such dynamic force—my grandfather.

" 'Big Daddy,' as we called him, had died two years previously. Though he had always ruled his family with an iron hand, Peter and all six of his children idolized him.

"The message, in unbending, formal language, was quite typical of him:

" 'I am glad to greet you. We, who have gone before, live. We love the ones who were dear during the earth life and are waiting to welcome you into a life of sympathetic understanding that lies beyond what you erroneously term death.'

"Now here's the oddest thing about the incident: the message ended with the word 'Hi-Hi.' Now that was the sign-off signal that all the Gaty boys had used when they were operating their own 'ham' radio station. Theirs was one of the first such stations in operation, and the sons— Theodore (my father), Lewis, Jack and Clint—had learned the Morse code almost with their ABC's. Uncle Jack, at 16, had been a radio operator on a sub chaser during the first World War.

"Peter was quite accustomed to psychic phenomena and it didn't disturb her in the least. She was the only one who ever saw the ghost of the 'McGonigal'—that was what we called the tall, squarish desk, which was as big as an old-

125

fashioned wardrobe. It had been made by a Mr. McGonigal for my great-grandfather, Samuel Gaty, and was kept in the North Room, along with a portrait of Samuel, during the period when we were doing the table-tipping.

"The 'McGonigal' was one of the prized possessions of Peter and Big Daddy when they were first married and had gone to live in St. Louis. It always had a prominent place in their living room.

"One Halloween Eve they were attending a party in St. Louis and someone started telling ghost stories. Peter—to Big Daddy's surprise—spoke up and said that she had 'a real ghost to talk about.'

" 'Does it scare you?' asked one of the guests.

" 'No,' Peter answered. 'He's a friendly ghost and keeps me company when I am alone. He doesn't appear all of the time; only occasionally—usually when I am busy dusting or straightening up the room—and then only if I glance at him from the corner of my eye and don't pay too much attention to him.'

" 'Can you describe him?' someone else asked.

" 'Yes,' Peter answered, smiling. 'He is very handsome; tall, with black hair, clean-shaven, but always with a slight blue shadow on his chin. He wears a white ruffled shirt, fitted coat and the sort of trousers that fasten under the shoes, at the instep—a sort of 1830 outfit, I should say.'

"Everyone started teasing Peter and she took it very well, but she wondered what Big Daddy would say. So far, he had made no comment. But on their way home in the carriage, he turned to her and asked, 'Do you know who you described perfectly this evening?'

" 'I have no idea,' Peter answered.

" 'You described Mr. McGonigal, the man who made our desk. He died when I was five years old, but I remember him—especially *the blue shadow on the chin.* He was a good friend of my father.'

"And Big Daddy was convinced that she *had* seen Mr. McGonigal! He had never talked with her about either the desk or Mr. McGonigal, and since Peter was fifteen years younger than he—and brought up in Minnesota—there would have been no chance of her ever having seen him in the flesh.

"There were lots of similar experiences in my family, but I think the most important one was when Daddy received a warning of his impending death—or, at any rate, what Mummy always believed was such a warning. (Daddy died in 1928, when I was two—and just a little over two years after his own father, Big Daddy, had passed on.)

"Again, the Gatys were engaged in table-tipping, and this time it was Daddy who was sitting by the window, taking down the messages as they were being rapped out—and again, in the dark.

"When the lights were turned on, Daddy read the message, and his face looked a little drawn. Then he laughed, and said, 'This is a lot of nonsense. It says here: *"Beware of a dead man by the stream."* '

"They tried again, hoping to get some other message that might clear up the mystery. But again the table rapped out the same words, 'Beware of a dead man by the stream.'

"Mummy was upset because she knew that we children liked to play near the stream, and finally voiced her fears.

" 'Teddy, you don't think this could mean that one of the children might be drowned, do you? I always worry so, when they play near the water.'

" 'Rubbish!' Daddy replied. 'It's probably the spirit of some old Indian that died down by the creek, that's all.'

"He crumpled up the message and stuffed it in his pocket, and suggested that they all forget it and turn in for a good night's sleep.

"Four months later, while mending a fence *down by the creek*, Daddy died instantly, of a heart attack.

"Mummy told us that he had gone for a physical check-up just a few days before that sinister message was received, and told her then that he was in fine shape. After the funeral, Mummy was too distraught to check with the doctor, and by the time she was herself again, the doctor had also passed on. So she was never able to learn if Daddy had received a warning from the doctor about his health. But she always felt that Daddy *did* know that the message was addressed to him, and what it meant."

KATE DRAIN LAWSON'S STORY

It is traditional, as observed elsewhere in this book, that wars always stimulate an interest in the supernatural, and more especially in the possibility of life after death. When normal media fail, troubled people are inclined to turn to clairvoyants, soothsayers and other minor prophets for answers to unanswerable questions. During World War I there was a tremendous revival of interest in ouija boards; manufacturers of such gimmicks had so many orders that they were obliged to greatly expand their plants.

This experience concerns a ouija board in wartime Paris, during the winter of 1917-18, when French morale was at its lowest ebb. The Germans had staged the first mass air raid in history—a pretty puny affair, in the light of what happened in World War II—but plenty terrifying then. The air raids soon became an almost nightly occurrence and all Paris knew that they were merely preliminary to the Germans' coming spring drive to capture the city itself. The only question was *when* it would occur.

A friend of mine, Kathryn Drain (better known now as Kate Drain Lawson, technical adviser on the Bob Hope TV show, and former director for the costume department of the Theatre Guild), who was stationed in Paris at the time, tells the story.

"I dashed off to Paris in July of 1917, very young and full of a holy zeal to save France all by myself, but also equipped with some Red Cross training which made me a useful Nurse's Aid at the old Ambulance No. 1 Hospital at Neuilly.

"At the time of the ouija board adventure, I had left the hospital and come to Paris to set up housekeeping for my father, Major James Drain, who was heading an

Allied commission for building tanks, which were then a new phase of military destruction.

"I found a charming furnished apartment in the rue Bayard, with rooms enough for us and several younger officers, as well as Dad's secretary. The apartment was filled with not-too-delicate Louis XVI furniture and the living room had a tiny fireplace, where we could augment the heat by burning charcoal—when we could get it.

"How a ouija board got into such a place is a rather amusing story. It had been borrowed from some Red Cross woman, who had brought it with her from the States.

"I had carefully stashed away the ouija board in a closet, for fear that Dad would come on it and scornfully ask what all the nonsense was about. We would only try to manipulate when he wasn't around. Now Dad, prior to his military service, was a hard-headed, clear-thinking lawyer. But he was also Irish, with imagination and a feeling for the imponderables. One night he arrived without previous warning and found us operating the board—and immediately became very much interested in the subject! From then on, he went to no end of trouble trying to find out what made it tick, and always with the idea of showing up trickery, if there were any, in its operation.

"As a ouija board operator, I proved to be something of a 'natural.' At least I take the bow, because it was only when I was one of the parties working the board that we got real results.

"We developed two 'familiars,' both purporting to be friends—in the spirit world—of one of the younger lieutenants who lived in our apartment. These two familiars were of vastly different character: one was a preacher who had known the lieutenant in his youth, whose 'conversations' were couched in dignified and scholarly language; the other was a former Army man, a young American who had enlisted with the Canadians before the United States got in the war and was killed while serving with an infantry outfit. His replies to our questions were rough, tough and frequently profane. He identified himself as one Monte Nicholls, described to us exactly how he had been killed and where. On checking, we learned that his statements were *completely accurate.*

129

"At a Christmas party, during the winter of 1917, we were operating the ouija board—myself and one other person—and someone asked the usual question: 'When will the German spring drive begin?'

"The ouija board answered glibly—if a ouija board can be said to be glib—'Eighty-four days from date.'

" 'But *when?*' one of the party persisted in asking.

"The tiny three-legged monitor that picks out the printed letters raced around the board like something possessed.

" 'Get a calendar!' it seemed to shout, 'I'm no book-keeper!' "

"When the laughter died down, someone did get a calendar and, counting the days, wrote down March 18 as the expected date of the German push. We all took note of this, and marked the date down in pencil on the back of the board.

"When spring came, most of our group had scattered to various assignments, taking them away from Paris, but Dad and I still made our headquarters in the rue Bayard and, whenever he could spare the time, he was an interested observer of the ouija board, asking it many military questions, for which the answers, if they came from any dependable military source, would of necessity be top secret.

"In March of 1918, the Parisians were subjected to one of the most harrowing experiences of the war. Mysterious explosions began taking place in various parts of the city, spaced at regular intervals. Since no planes could be seen over the city, sabotage was suspected, and the enigma became more baffling, as well as more frightening, with every recurrence. One explosion took place during a church service, badly damaging the church and killing a number of worshipers. All Paris was in a panic of apprehension.

"Three days after these explosions started—on March 21—the long-expected German offensive began. It then became apparent that the mystery explosions in Paris were part of the softening-up process, preliminary to the all-out drive. The French learned that they had been caused by explosions of shells fired by the Boches' latest lethal weapon, a giant gun which they had playfully named 'Big Bertha,' firing on Paris from forty miles away.

130

"So the ouija board had hit it almost on the nose. The actual attack on Paris, via the long-range gun, had started on *March* 18.

"This was not the only time that the board gave us a warning. During that dreadful spring of 1918, when Paris was constantly under bombardment, the ouija board would interrupt itself suddenly, in the midst of a sentence, to state that the planes would be over the city in *twenty minutes*— and they were! We had only time to pull the curtains and blackout the apartment before the *alerte* sounded.

"We kept records of all these ouija board 'conversations' and it was quite a voluminous mass. Dad had some idea of writing a book about these experiences after the war and Mother gathered all the material together, with the intention of having it copied off on the typewriter for him.

"Carl Montgomery was one of Dad's lieutenants, and much of the information we collected via the ouija board purported to come from his father, who had been a Senator from North Carolina. Judge Birney, who also entered into the 'conversations,' was also a great friend of my father. They frequently played golf together at the Washington Country Club; as a matter of fact, the Judge died of a heart attack while on the golf course. And there were *many discussions of golf* from the ouija board. But both men had been gravely concerned with the problems of the world and both were vigorous altruists, as many of the questions and answers indicated.

"One of our greatest difficulties with the ouija board was the speed it developed. It simply was not possible to catch the letters and write them down at the same time, so we usually had a friend sit by and write them down as we called them off. The words frequently ran together and no one knew what had been said until the letters were separated into words. Sometimes the board moved so rapidly that it would skip a word to two, *then go back and correct itself.*

"We experimented with blindfolding the operators, to prove that they were not manipulating the board visually —not by tying a little handkerchief over the eyes, but using a large Turkish towel, securely wrapped and tied so that only the tips of the noses were sticking out, to permit breathing! One evening, we turned the ouija board face down, while someone lay on the floor, looking upward at it, and called off the letters. But the board went blithely ahead with its messages.

"The bulk of our notes date from the spring of 1918. At the time, we checked as many details as we could and found that the board, while rather vague at times, *did not make mistakes*. Monte Nicholls was our most colorful 'correspondent,' and we were sometimes startled by the violence of his remarks. He was frequently impatient with us, and would break into the conversations between Dad and Senator Birney.

"Monte showed up again, this time in World War II, when I was aboard the West Point, the troopship that carried some nine thousand soldiers (and myself) to India in 1943. He also made an 'appearance' while I was out there. And here comes the most dramatic part of my story. It seems Monte and Dad had gotten together, in the spirit world, and there were several other old friends with them—friends whose acquaintance we had first made in Paris in 1918! Unfortunately, I kept no written proof of their messages.

"I have always been sorry that Dad died before he could get around to writing the book he had planned about our Paris experiences. It would have made an interesting contribution to supernatural literature."

THE WHITE HOUSE GHOST

It is a matter of record that Abraham Lincoln had a premonitory dream that occurred four times—three times prior to important Civil War battles, and a fourth time on the eve of his assassination. And it is one of Washington's most persistent legends that the spirit of Abraham Lincoln still hovers around the White House.

Why, out of all the great personages who have occupied that historic mansion, Lincoln alone seems to attach himself to the place, is anybody's guess. The professional psychics believe that it is because the Civil War President, who led such a tragic life, had died prematurely, leaving behind a great deal of unfinished business.

The story goes that when Carl Sandburg was preparing his epic biography of the Great Emancipator, he called on President Roosevelt and asked F.D.R. if he knew in just which one of the famous White House rooms Lincoln had spent most of his time. The President replied that he didn't *know*, but that he had always *felt* that it had been the Blue Room. He then suggested that Sandburg wander around the house and decide for himself, letting his intuition guide him.

Sandburg followed the President's suggestion and finally, after standing for some time beside the long windows of the Blue Room, which overlook the Washington Monument, he decided that F.D.R. was right.

The Lincoln Bedroom, as it has been identified ever since Lincoln slept there, is even more associated with his personality. While the Roosevelts were occupying the White House, a group of Broadway entertainers were being shown through the various rooms by Mrs. Eleanor Roosevelt in person. When they reached the Lincoln Bedroom, Patricia Bowman, the ballet dancer, remarked that she felt that the place was "haunted." Mrs. Roosevelt

133

smilingly admitted that she felt that way, too, and recalled with amusement an incident that had occurred just a few days before.

"I was sitting in my study downstairs when one of the maids burst in on me in a state of great excitement. I looked up from my work and asked her what was the trouble.

" 'He's up there—sitting on the edge of the bed, taking off his shoes!' she exclaimed.

" 'Who's up where, taking off his shoes?' I asked.

" 'Mister Lincoln!' the maid replied."

I printed this story in my Broadway column in the New York *Daily News*, and a short time later—apparently after being questioned about the incident—Mrs. Roosevelt elaborated on the Lincoln legend in her own newspaper column, "My Day." She also advanced her own theory that any place where someone had lived *hard* would be quite likely to be haunted by their personality—certainly as plausible a theory as any, concerning haunted houses.

THE METROPOLITAN OPERA GHOST

James Reynolds, the artist and onetime Broadway stage designer (no one who ever saw them has forgotten the beautiful sets he turned out for the *Greenwich Village Follies*), has written a number of good books about ghosts and haunted houses, superbly illustrated by himself.

After these books have come out, he told me, there has always been a tremendous amount of mail from readers unknown to him, volunteering their own personal experiences along this line.

One story Jimmy did not use, but which he assured me could be authenticated, concerned the Metropolitan Opera House ghost, or one of the ghosts—there must be many hanging around the august institution. However, you could hardly expect the Metropolitan Opera to *admit* such goings on! Here is the story as Jimmy told it to me.

Soon after the Met opened for the season, (Jimmy thinks it was sometime in 1955) a woman attended a matinee alone. She hadn't intended to be alone; the friend for whom she had bought the seat next to hers couldn't make it. So she sold the extra ticket back to the box office at the last minute.

She was considerably annoyed by the person who subsequently did occupy it. Her next seat neighbor was a robust woman, dressed in a silk outfit which rustled loudly every time she moved. She also rustled her program, apparently on purpose, and whenever the leading soprano was giving forth with an aria, she would nudge her neighbor in the ribs and hiss "flat, flat, *flat!*"

Shushing her proved of no use, so the first woman, irritated, finally got up and went outside to complain to the management. An usher was sent down to investigate. He returned to report that the seat next to the complainant was vacant and *had* been vacant *the entire perform-ance.*

Whether it was Jimmy's own conclusion isn't clear to me, but it seems the consensus of opinion of all who heard the story was that the ghost lady was the late Mme. Frances Alda, who had behaved that way when, as wife of director Giulio Gatti-Casazza, she could afford to do so. In any event, it was well known that, in that period of her life, she was given to attending performances of her rivals and audibly whispering "flat, flat, flat!" and doing other annoying things to break them up.

The oddest thing about the story is that the woman who did the complaining actually had black and blue bruises on her left arm for days afterwards!

ALICE VAN RENSSELAER THAYER'S STORY

One of the interesting and more curious phases of supernatural phenomena is the gift for speaking in strange languages which have never been studied or, so far as the subject knows, even heard. There are many such cases on record.

Alice Van Rensselaer Thayer (at one time married to the late Count Louis Montgomery) told Buell Mullen that when she was a small child she had known a little verse, which she had frequently recited. Her family, and everyone else who heard it, mistook it for some childish gibberish, and she herself had no idea where she had picked it up. Though she had spent most of her early years abroad, mostly in Paris, and spoke French fluently, she had never met any Russians, nor, so far as she knew, had she ever heard Russian spoken.

While still in her teens, Miss Thayer was invited to a dinner party in Paris and found that her table companion was an attractive and charming gentleman, a Russian.

Their conversation somehow turned to the subject of childish fantasies, that world of unreality in which so many young people dwell, and to which they can never return once they have grown away from it.

In this connection, Miss Thayer mentioned the language which she apparently had created for herself and which no one else understood, which she herself didn't understand, for that matter, being merely intrigued with the sounds. She then recited the little verse of "gibberish."

Her table companion was astonished.

"You are quoting a verse written by one of our major Russian poets—Lermontov," he said. "It is a poem dealing with reincarnation."

And then, as if that weren't surprising enough, he added: "And I would like to congratulate you on your *unusually good Russian accent!*"

SPOOKS ANONYMOUS

Innumerable stories have come to me to which, unfortunately, no names can be attached. Although the teller of the story assured me in every case that it was entirely true, for one reason or another he did not want to be identified with it in print.

An actress who had been a featured performer during the heyday of vaudeville and did considerable traveling "on the road," had numerous experiences in connection with her work. One experience that wasn't amusing at all occurred to her in a Midwestern city.

Bunty, as we'll call her, checked into a hotel near the theater where she was to appear and had her trunk sent up before she had inspected the room. When she got around to unpacking her trunk, she removed several gowns and walked across the room to the clothes closet, intending to hang them up.

She opened the clothes closet door and started back in horror at the sight that greeted her eyes—a woman's body, quite dead, hanging by the neck from a closet hook.

Bunty slammed the closet door, ran to the phone and called for the desk clerk to come upstairs, on the double quick. He arrived, quite breathless from running upstairs to save time. Bunty was so speechless from shock that she could only point to the closet door. The clerk opened the door—and there was absolutely nothing in the closet.

Bunty then told him what she had seen and the clerk listened with (as she described it) "beads of perspiration standing out on his forehead." He continued to stare at her incredulously for a few minutes, then he said: "It happened last week. A woman committed suicide by hanging herself in that closet. Please say nothing about it to anyone. I will get you another room immediately."

An insurance salesman writes:

"Don't expect me to vouch for this: it sounds like one of those old wives' tales that Alexander Woollcott loved to tell on the radio, but this is the way it came to me.

"Two women were recently motoring up to West Point to call on a cadet—a son, or nephew, or something—when they were stopped on Route 9-W by a hitch-hiker. He was a little, thin man, middle-aged and respectable-looking, so they decided to stop and give him a lift. He turned out to be a pretty gabby passenger, and they were both glad when, a few miles farther up the road, he asked to be put down.

The little old man was quite voluble in his thanks, saying that he wished he knew some way by which to return the courtesy.

" 'Perhaps I can—now,' he added. 'You see, ladies, I have a psychic gift. I can tell you that within three hours there will be a dead man in your car; also that in January a prominent European politician will be shot—not killed, mind you, just shot.'

"The women, convinced that the old man was a lunatic, drove on. An hour later they were stopped on the Storm King Highway by a state trooper. There had been a bad smash-up on the road and the trooper asked them to take one of the victims, a man, to the nearest hospital. When they arrived at the hospital, the interns came out to get the man, but he was dead on arrival.

"Don't ask me to make good on the rest of the story. At that time—or now, for that matter—*any* European politician is likely to get shot."

A Broadway press agent tells me that in his youth, spent in Syracuse, New York, he and several cronies were given to saving up their money and attending the local vaudeville theater in a group.

One bitterly cold and windy night, they were walking up the street from the theater after the show, when suddenly, from an alleyway, a white figure with clutching arms came toward them. The figure was so realistic that they were frightened out of their wits and started to run. The mystery man in white continued to pursue them for about half a block, but appeared bent on clutching *one particular boy.*

Suddenly the figure fell to the sidewalk, and they discovered that it was only a man's starched shirt that evidently had been blown off a clothesline from an alleyway. The wind had puffed up the shirt and spread the arms, and it had frozen solid in that shape.

The incident was reported, as an amusing item, in the local newspapers. Three days later the story was revived, but this time with a macabre twist. The lad whom the ghostly shirt apparently had sought to embrace was killed at a railroad crossing, not a stone's throw from where the incident of the shirt occurred.

A woman writer of pulp fiction—love stories, not ghost stories—told me that several years ago she was invited to spend a week end in Connecticut at the house of a friend. It was one of those charming old New England houses, "done over."

The writer, whom we'll call Marian, had attended a party in Greenwich Village the night before—quite a drinking party, as it turned out—and she arrived at her Connecticut destination with a shattering hangover.

A servant took her bag upstairs and Marian sat down in the living room with her hostess, Mrs. B., to catch up on gossip. After a time, she remarked that she desperately needed an aspirin, and would like to go upstairs and get one out of her bag. Mrs. B. said she would have one brought to her, but Marian said she also wanted to get something else out of her bag, and her hostess told her to look in the first room on the right at the top of the stairs.

She entered the room and was startled to find it already occupied. In the center of the room was a large, four-poster bed, and in the center of the bed was an old woman, sitting up and clutching the bed covers. The expression on her face was one of terrified surprise and, as Marian expressed it, "sent chills down her spine."

Marian murmured, "I beg your pardon," and backed out of the door. To herself she was thinking, "How odd that Mrs. B. didn't tell me that the room was occupied." However, she did need to get to her bag, so she tapped on the door, again said "I beg your pardon," and gently pushed the door open.

This time the room was not occupied. There was no four-poster bed, no terrified old lady. Twin beds occupied the same space, with smart, modern chintz covers. Her bag was lying on a luggage rack, at the foot of one of the beds. She opened it and located the aspirin bottle, thinking to herself that the apparition she had just witnessed could just possibly be blamed on her hangover.

When she rejoined her hostess downstairs, she described her experience. Her hostess smiled quite understandingly.

"Oh, we see that old lady around here all the time—upstairs, downstairs, on the stairs. It's quite a story. It seems she once owned this place and there was a bitter dispute among her relatives over the matter of who had prior rights, in the matter of inheritance. For years some of them tried to take it away from her, legally, and she lived in mortal terror—afraid that, having failed to dispossess her, they might resort to more violent means.

"Please don't say anything about it in front of the servants. More than one has quit us because of that old dame."

The wife of a well-known and successful author, who'll have to be identified here as Walter Beiner (there's no such name, so far as we know), told me about a spook who almost broke up her marriage and might have resulted in her being packed off to a mental institution. He was, she said, one of her husband's dead relatives—dead, however, a long, long time.

It all started, she told me, during a casual session of table-tipping in Europe with a group of friends, whom she didn't name, since they do not figure in the story.

The messages directed to her purportedly came from an ancestor of her husband, a soldier during the Revolutionary War who apparently was no better than he

141

should be, and frankly admitted it. He had, in fact, been hanged as a horse thief, or worse. His one virtue, he boasted, was that he was truthful, and he insisted that if Mrs. Beiner would look up the records when she returned to the States she would find that his story was factual. In every "conversation" he was insistent on one thing: she must never mention him, in any way, to her husband.

When Mrs. Beiner did return to this country, she did considerable research and discovered that Enoch, as he had called himself, was an actual character in Revolutionary history. By now, he was giving his messages via automatic writing, a talent that Mrs. Beiner had acquired as an outcome of the original table-tipping sessions. She was, incidentally, acquiring a first-hand report on many early American affairs which might serve as the nucleus of a book. Many times, she was tempted to tell her husband about all this, but held to her "agreement" with Enoch not to do so.

This went on for quite a while. Eventually, the Revolutionary spook got around to telling her that if she would obey instructions *implicitly*, he would eventually "materialize" for her—but always with the injunction that she was not to confide in her husband.

Among the family heirlooms of the Beiner family was a pewter plate. Enoch told Mrs. Beiner that if she would lie down quietly on the bed, relaxed and with her hands crossed on her bosom, and continue to look at the plate—propped up at the footboard of the bed—she eventually would be able to see his face. He was quite specific about the date and the time when she should do this.

As it happened, on the date and the time named, Mr. Beiner was at home, and his wife realized that it would take a bit of doing to follow out Enoch's instructions without her husband being aware that something unusual was going on.

It was early evening, following the dinner hour. Mr. Beiner was sitting in the living room, reading, while Mrs. B., feigning a headache, lay down in the bedroom next door. She had dimmed the lights—per instructions—and propped the pewter plate up at the footboard, where she could gaze into it.

She continued to stare fixedly at the plate for the better

part of an hour and had become so drowsy that she feared she would fall asleep, so decided to give up the experiment. Then she glanced at her hands.

In the place of her own white and well-manicured hands were two large, rough, hairy and repulsive hands of a man! Mrs. Beiner gave a shriek of terror and leaped off the bed, knocking the pewter plate to the floor.

Her husband, startled out of his wits by the outcry, rushed into the bedroom to find his wife almost in a state of hysteria. She then blurted out the whole story.

Mr. Beiner was furious. He upbraided her for following up such an idiotic suggestion and demanded that she give up all such experiments, including the automatic writing, and try and forget the whole business as quickly as possible—which, of course, she was only too glad to do.

But, as King James put it, "who sups with the devil should have a long spoon." Mrs. Beiner was quite willing to part company with her husband's Revolutionary ancestor; but not so on his side. From then on, constantly, and usually in the dead of night, she would be disturbed by violent rappings on the headboard of her bed. In terror, she would awaken her husband, but he could *never hear the sounds.*

By now, the frantic woman was about ready to submit herself to a psychiatrist, or get herself committed—and her exasperated husband was on the point of agreeing with her that some such drastic action should be taken.

On a visit to Los Angeles, she decided to pay a call on the aging poet, Ella Wheeler Wilcox, who, she understood, was much interested in spiritualistic phenomena. She told the story to Mrs. Wilcox, and when she reached the point in the story about the promised physical materialization, a violent rapping was heard in the room. To Mrs. Beiner's intense relief, Mrs. Wilcox also heard the rappings, and she (Mrs. Beiner) decided that she wasn't going crazy, after all.

It was the last time the Revolutionary spook troubled her.

"I don't know whether this comes under the classification of 'supernatural' or not, but I'll let you be the judge.

143

At any rate, it was a first-hand experience that left a lingering suspicion in my mind that there must be something to this 'extra-sensory perception' stuff, after all."

The speaker was a New York newspaperman who asked that his name not be used.

"I'll have to preface this story with an explanatory line about myself and my early background.

"As you know, a great many children live in a sort of dream world of their own, and frequently suffer from delusions of grandeur. They are convinced inside of themselves that they don't belong to the parents who acknowledge them as their own, but to people far more important —and, preferably, royalty. It is probably one form of escapism, but anyway it is a well-known phenomenon.

"I was just such a kid. My family was very poor and we were living in a godforsaken hamlet down south, all of which I resented intensely. I was only about eight at the time and frequently left to my own devices because I was a sickly youngster and couldn't go out and do much fishing, or play baseball, or indulge in the activities of my older brothers.

"On the front porch of our frame house we had a small rope swing, and I used to sit in it and swing, and daydream by the hour. I vividly remember one daydream because of its rude awakening. In my mind, I was a little prince, walking across a greensward—what the French call a *tapis vert* —somewhere in France. How I ever got the notion of being in France, I'll never understand. No members of my family had ever been in France, so far as I know; I had never seen any pictures of that country, and had never heard a word of French spoken. Being of Scotch-Irish extraction, I could hardly credit it to inherited race memory. It might have been reincarnation, of course, but no one had heard of Bridey Murphy at that time.

"Anyway, in my daydream, I was walking across the greensward and away from a line of stables—low, gabled buildings of whitewashed brick, with dovecotes. I was looking backward over my shoulder to see if anyone was laughing at me. I had just fallen off my pony and felt I had lost face. I distinctly remember the clothes I was wearing —a riding habit of dark blue velvet, with pants that came slightly below the knee, more or less in the fashion of the Charles II period.

144

"Just about this time, the old and rotten rope of the swing broke and the back of my head hit the floor with a loud thump, raising a good-sized lump. I guess that is what sort of fixed that particular daydream in my mind.

"Twice in my life, that daydream has come back to me, each time when I was in some low state of mind, which might confirm my theory of escapism.

"The fourth time the dream came back to me was under decidedly different circumstances.

"After Prohibition was repealed, you may remember, the New York *Telegram* promoted a series of columns by Selmer Fougner titled 'The Wine Trail.' The theory was that New Yorkers, after so many years with bathtub gin and other forms of hootch, would again learn to drink 'decently and in order,' and go in for the better types of wines and liqueurs. Fougner, I believe, was a Swiss, and affected the title 'Baron'; in fact, he used it in his by-line. He was celebrated as a gourmet, and because of the publicity he gave the wine people, was on the receiving end of a practically unlimited supply of the best wines.

"To use up the wines—as well as to promote them among his top-drawer acquaintances—the Baron used to give an annual dinner party in his apartment, with Mrs. Fougner acting as hostess. I don't know who did the actual cooking, but those meals were superlatively prepared and sumptuously served. And, naturally, the right wines went with every course.

"I happened to be invited to one of those dinners, and though I knew the guests were a distinguished lot, I didn't catch many of the names. I certainly did not catch the name of the gentleman who figures in this story.

"After dinner, coffee was served in the living room. Then someone suggested playing a parlor game that reminds you of those 'mind-reading' experiments at Duke University. One person was to go back into the dining room, close the folding doors, and remain there until called back. Meanwhile, those in the living room were to decide on some name—of person, place or thing—and concentrate on it. When they had all firmly fixed their minds on this subject, the party in the dining room was invited to return, and asked to guess what was on their minds. As I remember it, the average of successful guessing was quite high; about one in every three, in some cases.

145

"When the interest in this particular parlor game seemed to wane, I remarked that I could do a pretty good trick of mind reading myself. Now this was pure exhibitionism—not escapism—and pure bluff, in any case. But they all fell for it and were eager to see me demonstrate.

" 'Blindfold me,' I said, 'and then someone turn me around three times, so that I won't know in which direction I am facing. Then I will tell *one* thing each to three people in this room.'

"They followed instructions, tied a handkerchief over my eyes, and turned me around slowly three times. Meanwhile, I was thinking very fast, about how I was going to make good.

"I decided just to utter the first thing that came into my mind, and the first thing that did come into my mind, for no reason whatsoever, was that daydream of my childhood which I have described. And it came back to me as vividly as a picture.

"By now, of course, I couldn't possibly know in which direction I was facing, but I went boldly ahead: 'In this corner,' I said, pointing in some direction that I couldn't see, 'there is a gentleman who fell off a pony when he was eight years old. He wasn't damaged but his feelings were hurt because he thought the grooms were laughing at him. He recalls the incident very well. He was wearing a riding habit of dark blue velvet, cut along the King Charles II lines. This happened in France . . .'

"I was interrupted by the voice of a man.

" 'Do you mind if it were a *green* velvet riding habit?' he asked. 'The rest of it is correct.'

"I had hit the jackpot on my first try, and I don't remember what I told the other two people. I do remember how astonished I was, when they took off my blindfold, to learn the identity of the gentleman who had spoken up. He was Count René de Chambrun, a descendant of Lafayette!

"Because of his distinguished ancestor, Count de Chambrun has the privilege of dual citizenry; he can claim to belong either to France or the United States. And since his mother was a sister of the late Nicholas Longworth, he speaks English as well as French.

"As I have stressed, it was pure bluff on my part, but from what I have read of those Duke University experiments with extra-sensory perception, I feel that my experience legitimately belongs in that category."

A prominent woman publisher of my acquaintance told me, after I'd known her for some time, that her life "had been peppered with oddments of psychic phenomena and extra-sensory-perception incidents," and, to this day, ever so often she is amazed to be again confronted with signs that she is seeing or hearing "beyond the expected," so to speak.

"I heard about my first experience of this kind," she told me, "long before I understood what it meant. My mother used to love to tell about the surprising thing I told old Dr. Smith one night when I was four years old, while walking home from church with him: *so* surprising a thing that he could hardly wait until I'd got to bed, to tell it to my parents.

"It was a beautiful moonlit night, and I was very happy. Dr. Smith was the treasurer of our church, and had allowed me, for the first time, to stay after service and separate the pennies, nickels, dimes and quarters of the evening's collection into their proper categories, while he was counting the bills. My parents had gone on ahead, and he walked me home when we were through with our interesting work. And this is how our conversation went, I am told:

" 'Isn't it a beautiful night,' he remarked. 'And such a fine round moon over—'

"Whereupon, I am told, I interrupted him by saying ecstatically, 'Oh, yes! And we are both *old souls*—and kindred spirits!'

"Mother always laughed, as she described how pale he was when he burst into the living room. He fidgeted until I'd gone upstairs and then said, almost in a whisper, 'Do you know, I was just getting ready to *say* just that: that we were both "old souls, and kindred spirits!" I had read it in a book, just this morning. How could she have known it! It's almost like *mind reading!*'

" 'Oh, yes,' Mother replied, a little unstrung. 'She *does* do that sometimes. I don't know *how*, but she does.'

"This sort of thing happened ever so often, and I used

147

to make quite a few people feel fairly eerie, during my childhood, by finishing their sentences for them, when I couldn't possibly have known what the endings were to be. It was at least twenty years later for instance, that I first heard, to understand, the meaning of an *old soul*—which seems to mean, in some esoteric faiths, one who is over-wise, and has lived before. I eventually learned not to say what I knew; it was too uncomfortable for everyone concerned.

"But the next *really* uncanny thing was the first time, many years later, that I heard a voice that wasn't there. . . . My husband, standing right beside me, did not hear it at all. We had just come from visiting my mother and father, in a town fifty miles away. Both were in excellent health and gay spirits, and we'd had a happy time. Just as we reached the dark foyer of our apartment house and were putting the key in the door, I heard a voice call me by name and say, 'Your father is dying.' I gasped in astonishment and said, 'John! Did you hear that? My father is dying!'

" 'Nonsense,' he said, 'why, he was *fine* when we left him. What gives you such an idea?' And, naturally, he pooh-poohed the idea that I'd heard any such thing. But when we reached our third-floor apartment, the phone was ringing loudly and persistently. When I answered it, my mother was sobbing, and she said, 'You'd better come right back. Your father has had a stroke. I've sent for the girls.'

"He lived for two more days, but never regained consciousness.

"But the most unnerving, most senseless manifestation of all—and the most recurring—was one that always bothered me at times when the tensions of my hectic life were already almost more than one person could handle. During the depression of the thirties, I worked as a salesperson in a bookshop: long hours, low pay and hard work, and my household had to be managed in my out-of-work hours. For several years it was a haze of passing days, weeks, months—all of them a reaching for the time when life would be simpler, happier. It was a time with me (as with millions!) of feeling over-extended in every direction. Feeling 'neon,' I used to call it . . . as if the fluid that runs in those bubbling neon lights ran in my veins instead of blood.

"It was always at the tensest of these times that the especially irritating *thing* happened. Sometimes I would not be aware of it. Proof of this came one day when I was requested to go to the superintendent's office. This was always a dread thing—to be called to the superintendent's office. He was a severe, even cruel man, with no softening overtones anywhere in his composition. And in those days of no jobs, such a summons could terrify.

'Now what have I done!' I scolded myself, on my way up to the office.

" 'Mrs. H.!' he roared as I entered. 'Do you want to *keep* your job?'

"Foolish question, indeed! I *had* to keep my job. 'I certainly do, Mr. S.,' I stammered. 'What have I done that is *wrong?*'

" 'You're doing *that thing* again,' he shouted back. 'You *know* it makes the customers nervous . . . and I don't understand it atall, atall,' he ended in a puzzled way. 'How can you *do* it? What *makes* you do it?'

"Then I knew. I'd been doing *that* again! Oh, Lord . . . It made me nervous, too.

" 'I'm terribly sorry, Mr. S.,' I said abjectly. 'I didn't know I'd been doing it lately. . . . I really will watch . . . you'll see—' and he growled something like 'See that you do!' and waved me out of the royal presence.

"What I had been doing—and did frequently at such times and didn't even *know* I'd been doing—was to write down the customers' names and addresses on the sales slips in my order book . . . *before they told them to me!* Complete strangers, standing wide-eyed and uneasy before me, because more often than not it was suddenly apparent that I had known their names and addresses even before they approached me to select their books!

"An odd, unnerving talent, that one. One I could do without. And, sure enough, every time I feel it coming on —as when I'm in an elevator and can anticipate a complete stranger's conversation with his or her companion and be quite right—I know I'm in for a nervous few weeks on one score or another.

"And then there's the time a voice saved me from taking

149

a certain plane that was lost in the mountains of Utah, but that's a fairly frequent psychic phenomenon. It's nothing like as off-beat as this names-and-addresses thing. But it is more useful, at any rate. Because of it I'm still here, sitting in restaurants suddenly knowing what somebody will say. And sitting in my office expecting an author who hasn't said a revealing word on the phone, yet knowing already exactly the subject of the book he wants to do for me.

"And the thing is—I'm almost always right."

SOME SPOOKY SETUPS

Murder apartments, meaning those dwelling places where people have been foully done to death, are in great demand in New York. This has nothing to do with this city's chronic housing shortage: it is merely a phase of the exhibitionism which seems to motivate so large a portion of society today. So eager are some people to bask in the white light of publicity that they actually *prefer* to live in a house that may have but recently dropped with human gore. It is a good conversational starting point for their cocktail guests! And it would not be surprising if such places harbored a few special ghosts.

When the Wayne Lonergan murder broke on the front pages of the newspapers, in all its grim and repellent details, the owner of the building where the crime occurred, was bewailing his bad luck in having sublet his personal quarters to the young Canadian Air Force man and his pretty wife Patricia (Patsy), whose skull was cracked by her husband, supposedly in a fit of jealous rage, using the owners' highly prized Empire candlesticks to do the job.

Said owner, Chester Fentriss, a longtime friend of my family—actually, he was my sister's singing teacher—was fearful that the notoriety would impair the value of his real estate.

"Quite the contrary," I assured him. "Your difficulty now will be fighting off a mob of applicants for the apartment."

And so it turned out to be. Between five and six hundred people rushed in to rent the place. The couple that finally got it, paying a very fancy price, were socially prominent and well-to-do people who could afford almost any quarters they might have chosen. They *wanted* to live in the Lonergan murder flat—and they wanted nothing about it changed!

151

It wasn't always thus. In a more conservative era, property owners did all they could to obliterate traces of a violent crime. Numbers on doors were altered, a redecorating job was immediately ordered and, usually, some relative was installed in the premises until the notoriety had died down and prospective tenants had forgotten about the sinister background of the address.

Back in the 1920's, when I was trying to make a living as an actor, I was asked by a woman friend, Edith Kinkead, to occupy her apartment temporarily while she was absent from the city on a business trip. The apartment, consisting of a living room, bedroom, bath and kitchenette, was located on the top floor of a converted brownstone on West 57th Street, in the same block with Carnegie Hall. It was exactly suited for its purpose, that of an astrology studio. The location was convenient, the neighborhood desirable, and the price much under what one would expect to pay, considering all these assets. Mrs. Kinkead admitted that she was surprised at the low rental, but decided she had better let well enough alone and not inquire the reason, if any.

She rearranged the apartment better to suit her own purposes, transforming the living room into a studio sleeping room, and using the bedroom as a small office. The two rooms were separated by glass doors, and one passed through the living-bedroom to get to the office.

Among the first clients was a man, a stranger, whom she asked to step into her office and close the doors, while she was dismissing another client in the outer room. While she was still talking, the man emerged from the office, remarking that it seemed "very stuffy" inside. Mrs. Kinkead suggested that he open the window, but the stranger declined, saying that he would take a short walk outside and return later. He did return, and this time elaborated on his first remark by saying that he had felt quite "suffocated" in the smaller room, and added that he felt that someone must have *actually been suffocated* there at some previous time.

His remark led Mrs. Kinkead to make some inquiries of the building superintendent, who informed her, rather reluctantly, that her studio apartment had been the former "love nest" of Dot King, the beautiful Broadway Butterfly —as the tabloids dubbed her—whose murder had been a seven-day sensation in the 1920's and still remains one of New York's most intriguing "unsolved" crimes.

Dot King had been done to death *by suffocation* in that room, after a furious struggle, her exquisitely beautiful blonde bobbed head buried beneath a pillow that had been saturated with chloroform.

Mrs. Kinkead had told me about the background of the apartment at the time she requested me to occupy it, during her trip to Chicago. A maid would look after the place, and my sole obligation would be to answer the phone mornings, to take business telephone messages, and to feed and water her pet canary, also seeing that it was covered up for the night.

During my brief tenancy, I felt nothing sinister about the outer room; if there were any hangover of "atmosphere" from the previous occupant, it was that of late, wild drinking parties. The canary apparently got the message, too, as it invariably woke up, and though its cage was thoroughly covered, started chirping around 3:00 A.M.—which, incidentally, was about the hour that the police believed Dot King had died.

During this interim, I was attending an after-theater supper party in the Gramercy Park section of New York, which is a long way from West 57th Street. It was a bitterly cold evening and, warmed by the open wood fire and several scotch-and-sodas, I remarked that I would prefer spending the rest of the night stretched out on the fireplace rug, rather than returning to my present diggings.

"Why?" my hostess inquired. "Aren't you comfortable there?"

"Oh, comfortable enough," I answered, "only it's not my own apartment, and—" I hesitated to go on. "Well, there's something *about* the place, the atmosphere of the place—"

"Come, come!" my hostess demanded. "Out with it! What's wrong with the place?"

"Well," I answered, somewhat shamefacedly, "it happens to be the apartment where Dot King was murdered. She was known as the Broadway Butterfly, but"—I added quickly—"it's a *canary* that keeps me awake."

When the general laughter had died down, another guest, a young man sitting by the fireplace who, as the saying goes, up to this time had taken no part in the conversation, spoke up.

153

"That's odd," he said. "I am living in one of those old brownstone jobs up in the West 70's. My apartment is one of those wickie-up affairs of one-room-bath-kitchenette that has been carved out of what must have once been an elegant drawing room, with paneled walls and all the things that once went into private mansions.

"The whole place has obviously seen better days and is desperately in need of repair, but I get the flat for such absurd rental that I decided not to complain. However, the other day I did confront my landlady and asked why she didn't do something about fixing up the place. 'At least,' I said, 'you could go so far as plugging up some of the holes in the woodwork. This, for example,' and I pointed out a hole in the frame of the door that led into the hall.

" 'Listen, young man,' the old girl replied, rather tartly, 'there's a law in this state that forbids you to destroy any evidence in an unsolved murder case. That is a bullet hole.'

" 'A bullet hole?'

" 'Yes, a bullet hole. And this, for your information, is the room where Mr. Elwell was shot.' "

So here we were, two strangers, occupying two of the most famous "murder apartments" in New York!

Mr. Elwell, in case you don't remember, was the famous bridge and whist expert, whose fatal shooting, by party or parties unknown, has never been solved. The pajama-clad body of Joseph Bowne Elwell was found early one morning by his housekeeper, seated bolt upright in his luxuriously furnished drawing room, with a forty-caliber bullet drilled through his forehead. The bullet went straight through his skull and penetrated the woodwork behind. And this was the bullet hole that the young man's landlady objected to filling up!

I am sorry I didn't get a chance to ask the stranger if the ghost of Mr. Elwell was still hovering about.

It was in another New York apartment, in another part of town, that I did blunder onto a clue which, to my own satisfaction, at least, does help to clear up one of the most baffling mysteries of our time—the murder, or at any rate, the disappearance of Agnes Tufverson.

I was visiting with the Floyd Macks, who then lived on East 22nd Street. Floyd for many years has been the narrator and announcer for NBC's famed "Telephone Hour." Our conversation somehow turned on the great number of unsolved crimes in New York.

"I am always amused, and just a little annoyed," I was saying, "at radio and television whodunits in which a murder case is glibly solved by some newspaper reporter who breezes onto the scene and, by some hocus-pocus of sleuthing understood only by scriptwriters, instantly picks the murderer and immediately solves the crime.

"I have never been called on to solve a crime, and I doubt if any other columnist has. However, like practically every other human being, I enjoy trying to dope it out. And one of the most interesting angles in so many cases is the imponderable—call it psychic, supernatural, or what you will—that enters into their solution; in other words, clues that are *blundered* onto. Take the Lindbergh kidnaping, for instance. Why should an unsuspecting truck driver, casually answering the call of nature, have blundered onto the corpse of the baby, which thousands of the best-trained detectives and criminologists, as well as a huge part of the civilian population, had been seeking for weeks?

"I think if detectives paid more attention to these 'imponderable' clues, they would get further in solving so many unsolved crimes—the Elwell murder, the Dot King murder, the disappearance of Agnes Tufverson, and a hundred others."

"And what about the Agnes Tufverson case?" Floyd Mack asked. "Could you brief us on that?"

"Yes. I've read a lot about it, and here is the story:

"Agnes Tufverson was an emotionally frustrated woman lawyer who, after a lifetime of hard work and self-denial, to educate herself and four younger sisters, took time out for a vacation that was to prove her undoing. This was in the spring of 1933. Agnes, the daughter of a Swedish immigrant, was by now a well-to-do and highly respected lawyer for the Electric Bond and Share Company of New York. She bought herself a round-trip tourist-class ticket for her first visit to Europe. Agnes, now forty-five, had

155

never married and, so far as her relatives and close friends knew, had never indulged in a romance or emotional experiences of any kind.

"Somewhere abroad—or possibly on shipboard en route home—Agnes made the acquaintance of a handsome, dashing character, about ten years her junior, who claimed to have been a Bulgarian who had served as a cavalry officer in the Austro-Hungarian Army, Ivan Ivanovitch Poderjay (pronounced po-der-hai) by name.

"Learning through conversation that Agnes had a nest egg of around $55,000, Poderjay followed her to New York and attempted to get her financially interested in promoting one of his inventions, a patented lock. Agnes declined, so, failing in this, Poderjay returned to Europe and cabled her, asking a straight-out loan of $2,500. This she also refused. So Poderjay returned to New York and, after a whirlwind courtship, married her.

"The ceremony took place at the Little Church Around the Corner. There were no witnesses or invited guests— this because Poderjay claimed to be 'jealous' of Agnes' friends. Three days before the wedding, Agnes had resigned from her job with the Electric Bond & Share, stating that she was going on a European honeymoon. And after that, she said, she was going to settle down in England, on one of her husband's 'estates.'

"Two days after the ceremony, the hitherto cautious and conservative lawyer withdrew $7,000 cash from two of her bank accounts and gave it to her bridegroom, keeping only $15 for herself. A fortnight later, she disposed of her stocks and bonds, proceeds of which she also turned over to Poderjay. On his marriage certificate, Poderjay had sworn that he had never been previously married, but while his lovesick bride was passing over her life savings to him, he was immediately cabling the money to *another wife* in London.

"Agnes proceeded with her honeymoon plans, blissfully unaware that she had married not only a bigamist, but also a liar, a charlatan, a confidence man, and one of the most bizarre monsters in all criminal history.

"Once married, Poderjay moved into Agnes' apartment, where she retained the services of a part-time maid, Flora Miller. For the next two weeks, the newlyweds remained sequestered, emerging only to go on wild shopping sprees, also something new to the economical Agnes.

"She avoided friends, but those who did see her, quite accidentally, reported that she seemed 'radiantly happy.' Her maid thought otherwise. She said that the bride had frequently complained of violent stomach pains after drinking black coffee which Poderjay insisted on making for her himself.

"The wedding took place on December 4th. On the afternoon of the 20th of that month, Agnes and Poderjay set out in a taxi for the 'S.S. Hamburg,' due to sail at midnight. Trunks and bags were sent to the pier, and many presents and *bon voyage* messages to the popular bride were awaiting them there.

"On arrival, Agnes learned, to her exasperated astonishment, that Poderjay had made no reservations aboard ship!

"She gathered up her gifts and returned to the apartment with Poderjay in a taxi. The driver later testified that he had heard them quarreling violently on the way home.

"Next day, Poderjay made a number of decidedly unusual purchases in the neighborhood shops along Third Avenue: a great quantity of sleeping powders, many sheets of heavy brown wrapping paper, two hundred razor blades, and a surprisingly large supply of vanishing cream —remarking to each of the sales clerks that these things were hard to get in Europe. At a luggage shop, he purchased a good-sized old-fashioned type of trunk, insisting on immediate delivery.

"Flora Miller remained at the apartment until eleven o'clock that evening, then was dismissed by Mrs. Poderjay with instructions to return next day. Poderjay angrily countermanded this order, telling the maid not to report until the day *after* tomorrow. Flora recalled that Mrs. Poderjay was very much upset at the time.

"Flora was the last person ever to see Agnes again—alive or dead—with the exception of Poderjay. When she returned, as directed, she found Poderjay alone. He was rummaging through his wife's papers, which he ordered the maid 'in a threatening manner' to burn. When Flora asked about her mistress, he shouted angrily that she had gone to Philadelphia.

157

"By now thoroughly frightened, Flora made a hurried exit. In doing so, she stumbled against the three trunks she had helped pack and another trunk, a new one she had not seen before.

"Poderjay meanwhile had obtained a *single* reservation aboard the 'S.S. Olympic,' and at ten o'clock that night he left the apartment, riding down the freight elevator with the trunks. One of these he insisted on keeping in the taxi in which he was riding—Agnes' wardrobe trunk.

"When he reached the ship, Poderjay had three of the trunks put in the hold; the fourth, which was Agnes' wardrobe trunk, he had put in his cabin.

"Later testimony from the ship stewards indicated that Poderjay was in a specially jovial mood during the trip, frequently inviting them to sit down in his stateroom and enjoy drinks with him.

"What happened after that is a long and involved story. Briefly, Poderjay rejoined in London the wife he had previously married: one of the wives, to be exact, since he had married another woman on the Continent, also illegally, as it was later proven.

"The woman in London was one Marguerite Suzanne Ferrand, of French descent. La Ferrand, it later developed, was quite as much of a monster as Poderjay.

"Shortly after Agnes' departure, her sisters received a cablegram from London, supposedly sent by her, stating that she did not like the English climate and was leaving immediately for India. It was the last message ever received from the vanishing bride, and it was later learned that Poderjay had sent it, forging her name.

"Miss Tufverson's family became convinced that she had met with foul play, and called on the Missing Persons Bureau in New York, asking that they investigate. Detectives were sent overseas and they learned that the Ferrand woman was wearing Agnes' new clothes, also carrying her beloved briefcase, which Agnes had never previously let out of her sight. But there were no signs of Agnes herself.

"Trailing Poderjay and the woman to Vienna, police learned that they had to deal with not one but two monstrous specimens of humanity. Poderjay, who had made a business of preying on women, apparently had met his match in Ferrand. He was a masochist; she a sadist, of the most frightful nature.

"The Vienna apartment concealed a torture chamber, where the woman would chain Poderjay to the floor and beat and torture him savagely, in the most ingenious ways. Detectives came into possession of letters between them, ridiculing the unfortunate Agnes Tufverson. These letters revealed that Poderjay was possessed of four different personalities. By turn, in his warped imagination, he was the Ferrand woman's lover, her mistress, her servant, and a 'slave' who served them both. These letters, in French and English, were written in *four distinctly different handwritings!*

"While indulging himself in the role of a female, Poderjay had tortured himself in the most extraordinary and abominable ways, and there were equally incredible and horrible evidences of his pathologic insanity.

"New York police managed to extradite the Bulgarian "captain" from Vienna, after considerable delay because of international complications, and he was brought back to the States to stand trial for bigamy—the only charge that could be brought against him, since there was no proof of murder.

"Poderjay was found guilty on the bigamy charge and sentenced to five years in prison. This prison term was divided between Sing Sing and Auburn. There is no record of what happened during his incarceration, except that he had a fight with a fellow prisoner and had one eye gouged out.

"Poderjay told many stories, all conflicting, about what *might* have happened to the missing Agnes Tufverson, but he stoutly denied that he had done away with her. He was questioned many times by the then Assistant District Attorney, Lyon Boston, and during one of these sessions he lost his temper, leaped to his feet and with lightning speed aimed a blow at Boston's face with his heel; the attorney ducked just in time.

"At the end of his prison term, Poderjay emerged, still belligerently insolent and sneering openly at the police. He was deported to Europe and there is no record of his having ever been heard from since."

We had got this far in reviewing the Agnes Tufverson

case when my hostess asked, "And have *you* a theory of what became of her?"

"I certainly have—and it has just come to me this minute," I answered glibly.

"Most of the detectives hit on the probability that Agnes Tufverson was drugged to insensibility or death by the sleeping powders, and her body stuffed into the trunk that Poderjay took with him in his stateroom aboard the 'Olympic.' This was Agnes' wardrobe trunk, which was divided into compartments.

"A dead body wouldn't fit into a wardrobe trunk unless it was dismembered first. That is where the razor blades and the brown wrapping paper come in. But if Poderjay dismembered Agnes' body in the apartment, it stands to reason that there would have been bloodstains *somewhere*. Flora Miller certainly would have noticed them when she cleaned the place after Poderjay departed. Detectives searched the apartment thoroughly and could find none.

"Now, human blood leaves an indelible stain on almost anything that it touches—floors, walls, furniture, clothing, et cetera. It is even difficult to remove from the skin, as Lady Macbeth found out.

"Now here is where the vanishing cream comes in! A café chef once told me that when using garlic, he always greases his hands in advance, to prevent the odor from clinging to his skin. By the same token, he told me, a butcher, or anyone cutting up a body—animal or human—could avoid bloodstains by cold-creaming his hands thoroughly in advance. The cream washes off, removing other evidence with it. Poderjay evidently knew this.

"Now this is my theory: I think that Poderjay used the large quantity of vanishing cream purchased on Third Avenue to thoroughly grease not only his hands and wrists but *his entire body*. I am convinced, as the New England jury was in the Lizzie Borden case, that Poderjay committed the murder *in the nude*. Furthermore, it is my belief that he thoroughly greased the bathtub and other plumbing, so that it would not retain blood stains.

"After dismembering Agnes' lifeless body in the bathtub—the greased bathtub—Poderjay scraped the bones clean with the safety razor blades. Then he tossed the flesh down the apartment house incinerator. There were absolutely no traces of bones in the furnace, which the detectives examined thoroughly, so he must have wrapped them in neat packages in the wrapping paper bought for the purpose, and stored them in several compartments of Agnes' wardrobe trunk. Once at sea, he disposed of the packages by throwing them overboard, one by one. His stateroom, according to all reports on the case, had extra-large portholes."

By now, my hostess was staring at me, glassy-eyed.

"Do you know where Agnes Tufverson lived, at the time she disappeared?"

"No," I answered, "though I vaguely remember that it was somewhere in the East 20's."

"Well, for your information," my hostess went on, "she lived in this apartment house; in fact, *directly over your head!*"

It was my turn to stare.

Since then, I have read everything I could find that has been written about the Agnes Tufverson case. I have also talked with Lyon Boston, the Assistant District Attorney who translated the Poderjay letters and had questioned Poderjay when he was a prisoner. But neither he, nor anyone else, had ever put any stress on the *vanishing cream* which Poderjay bought such a quantity of—and which, I believe, enabled him to commit the "perfect crime."

Could it have been the uneasy spirit of Agnes Tufverson herself, still hovering around her former home, who had somehow given me the clue, as well as a very plausible solution of the crime?

SOME ROCKLAND COUNTY GHOSTS

Ghosts can be both pleasant and charming, and sometimes even possessed of a sense of humor. There seems to be quite a lot of this type up my way, in Rockland County, New York.

My friend Jane (Mrs. Clarence) Anderson, while doing research for an informal history of Rockland County, blundered onto quite a few of them. It was while seeking data on architectural curios that she learned even more curious things about Hudson Valley houses.

"In addition to the increased values in real estate that resulted from the influx of artists, actors, playwrights and authors in our community, there were other interesting developments," Mrs. Anderson writes. "The newcomers seem to have stirred up quite a number of ghosts. Reports started to come in of all sorts of odd manifestations.

"In a house in West Nyack, for example, the new owners became annoyed by a lady ghost who apparently objected to the radio being operated after 10:00 P.M. At exactly that hour, she would descend the stairs, her skirts rustling audibly as she came, and the entire living room soon became too chilly for comfort. If the family co-operated and switched off the radio, she returned upstairs, again rustling as she went, and the room again became pleasantly warm.

"In another house, near the Missionary Institute in Nyack, a ghost who had probably never enjoyed such conveniences, began to enjoy the new bathroom installed downstairs. The new owner would see the bathroom door quietly open, then firmly close. Then he would hear the sound of water running and splashing. A few moments later, the door would open again and there were no more sounds from the bathroom. Considerably annoyed, he

162

checked for draughts, and even called in the plumbers, but none of them could explain the phenomenon.

"In a house in Upper Grandview, what appears to be a mother and child ghost combination wake up the family every morning, quite early. From the sounds of paper being crushed, kindling wood snapped and coal poured on, it seems the mother ghost is starting a fire in the old range, although the old kitchen range was long ago thrown out and a new gas stove put in. Shortly after this ghostly fire is started, the smell of coffee starts rising through the house. And then the child ghost can be heard running around and apparently bouncing a little rubber ball!

"Then, on the Greenbush Road, in an old farmhouse—it is now the home of the artist, Whitney Hoyt—was the ghost of a very much annoyed old gentleman. It seems that one winter in the latter part of the last century, this man died, and his family gathered to bury him, first holding a wake over his coffin, which lay in the living room.

"But the day before the funeral was to take place, a blizzard came up, and snow banked the house so deeply that no one could get out of doors, even to get to the woodshed. The family used up all the wood that was in the house, then started breaking up the chairs and tables for firewood. Finally, they decided to burn the old man's coffin.

"This must have irritated the old gent because he—or his spirit—continued to stay on in the living room, exuding such a chill that the people who occupied the house later were never able to keep the room warm, despite a new furnace and an adequate heating system. They finally gave up, moved out and built themselves a modern house near West Nyack."

From other Rockland County residents come similar stories. The B. O. Jacobsens, who operate an antique shop in Nyack and live nearby, have had their own experience. Before moving into their present home, they occupied a much older house nearby, a brownstone dating from an earlier period. At one point in the early evening, almost as dependably as clockwork, Mrs. Jacobsen told me, the room would be pervaded by the odor of fresh apples, apparently borne in by unseen hands from the kitchen. Of course no one ever saw the bearer, but the impression was so strong that she was a vivid, buxom and kindly matron, that the family nicknamed her "Apple Annie."

The bulk of the County's ghosts, goblins and spooks— and "spook," by the way, is a Dutch word—seem to be inheritances from the early Dutch settlers. There is a highway known as Spook Rock Road with its own special legend—that of a young girl, sacrificed on the rock by Indians.

Carl Carmer, the Hudson River historian, thinks the Germans were there ahead of the Dutch, and some of the legends would seem to bear him out. The dwarfs playing ninepins amid the Wagnerian thunder of a Catskill storm do suggest the characters in the Nibelungen Ring. And the "storm ship" that reputedly sails the Hudson, full-rigged and flying the flag of the Low Countries—only to disappear in thin air among the Hudson Highlands— could be a local version of the *Fliegende Holländer*.

But it is about the High Tor legend that we are chiefly concerned.

Most New Yorkers—New York City dwellers, that is— had never heard of High Tor until a play of that name opened on Broadway during the season of 1937 and became an overnight hit. Maxwell Anderson, mystic, poet and playwright, and himself a resident of Rockland County, had fallen under the spell of the Tor and its legends and woven them into a play, which Guthrie McClintic produced. It was something of a neighborhood affair, since Burgess Meredith, the leading man, also resided in the County.

High Tor—the mountain, that is (Tor means a "lofty, jutting rock")—is only forty miles north of New York City, and though less than a thousand feet high, it dominates not only the countryside around it but also the history, folklore and legend. In fact, fewer promontories on the entire continent of North America are so richly endowed in that respect.

From the Tor's summit, the Indians sighted the sails of the Half Moon on Henry Hudson's first voyage of discovery. Where an electric beacon now warns voyagers in the sky, the prehistoric inhabitants once lighted their signal fires. Some of the myths of High Tor actually antedate the Christian era, and one of the more charming legends is that the Three Wise Men came here to build an altar to their newfound God.

Geologists claim that the Tor is, or was, actually, the oldest piece of land above water—not only on this continent, but on the entire globe, and was once higher than the Himalayas. The erosion of millions of years has cut it down, and is still wearing it away. Botanists have discovered on its rocky slopes varieties of desert cactus that disappeared from this region twenty thousand years ago.

George Washington is said to have mapped much of his Hudson River campaign from this eyrie, more especially the Battle of Stony Point, which made Revolutionary War history and established the fame, as well as the nickname, of General "Mad" Anthony Wayne—whose ghost, incidentally, is often reported seen by night-riders on the Storm King Highway, always astride his favorite horse. It was at the foot of the Tor, on the road that is still called the Long Clove, that Major John Andre met Benedict Arnold for their ill-fated rendezvous at nearby Treason House.

Quite a setting for spook stories!

Near the top of the Tor is a farmhouse, and it was around this farm and its fabulous owner, old Elmer Van Orden, that Max Anderson wove his drama, much of which was factual.

For years, Elmer Van Orden had waged a singlehanded fight to prevent his land from suffering the fate of nearby property. All around him was evidence of that fate. In a new erosion, not of nature, a traprock concern was gradually eating its way into the sides of the mountains and nearby palisades.

Van Orden, then in his seventies, was the last living inhabitant of the farm that had been deeded to his ancestors in the personal handwriting of King George III of England. Elmer could have sold his property and retired with a comfortable sum, but he loved the mountain where he

165

had spent his boyhood, exploring the Indian caves and the ruins of old Dutch houses, with the inevitable lilacs growing beside the red stone cellar.

He liked his way of life, and saw no reason to change it. The farmhouse where he lived, alone but for a hired "boy" named Gus Weltie—by now a white-haired man of sixty—had no electricity, no running water, nor any of the things we call modern conveniences. One chopped wood for their fires and fetched water from a spring sixty feet distant from the house. Provender was bought at the general store on South Mountain Road, a mile or more away.

Though keenly aware of the dramatic potentialities of Elmer's long fight with the traprock concern, Anderson also knew that it would have to be embellished for a stage plot. A romance was indicated, so he made Elmer, as his hero, a young man; he telescoped time and space and created the ghost of a little Dutch girl, dead three hundred years, who was in love with him.

Anderson had never met Elmer Van Orden, nor had he ever made the tortuous journey up the mountain to see the farm that his play eventually was to save. But his imagination served him better than he could have dreamed.

I, too, had known the story of High Tor, mostly through a friend, Hume Dixon, whose estate was on the road that skirts the lower slope of the mountain. On many a blustery winter night, beneath the great stone chimney of her converted eighteenth-century farmhouse, I had heard the legends of the countryside. And one that stuck in my mind was the story of the Dixons' own particular ghost. . . .

"I have seen her many times," Hume told me. "But always in one place—at the head of the stairs, standing in an attitude of welcome, and invariably smiling. She seems to be a young woman, dressed in some sort of linsey-woolsey material; the dress simply cut and gathered at the waist, with a full skirt. Her hair is a nondescript light brown, falling lightly around her shoulders—a sort of 'early American' hair-do, I would call it. Her best feature is her mouth; large, and always curved in a warm, generous smile.

"She has never bothered me in the least. I have grown quite accustomed to her, in fact, and in a lonely country house, her presence is almost welcome. Many times, when

I have been working late in my study, on the second floor, I was aware that she was just outside the door, standing, as usual, at the head of the stairs. Who she was, or what was her history, though, I have never been able to find out."

And there it might have rested but for Pearl Harbor and the Second World War. Mrs. Dixon, a volunteer civil defense worker, was assigned to canvass the neighborhood and learn what houses were available—naturally with plumbing and other facilities—for use by possible evacuees from New York City in the event of a bombing attack.

In company with a friend, Marie Louise Gaillard, she made the rather difficult journey up the Tor to question Elmer Van Orden about what his house had to offer. Her questions were answered, even before she asked them, by the primitive state of the farm. But she lingered on, glad to find an opportunity to talk to the old man.

"Elmer sat in an armchair, one foot bound up and resting on a Victorian stool," Mrs. Dixon told me later. "His mind seemed to be in that confused state that comes to some old people when their end is near. I didn't know how really sick he was, and certainly didn't know that I was to be his last caller, when I was there. Soon afterward, he was taken to the hospital and never returned.

"When Elmer died, he bequeathed a life tenancy of the farm to Gus, the 'hired boy.' And it later was saved from the fate he had dreaded by a committee that bought the surrounding land and gave it to the state, for a park. People everywhere contributed to the fund; kids raided their piggy banks to give. The Committee to Save High Tor included Maxwell Anderson, Guthrie McClintic, Burgess Meredith and members of the *High Tor* cast, as well as many other famous people."

Mrs. Dixon smiled, remembering her visit with old Elmer.

"I told him I lived on South Mountain Road, and described the house. He nodded his remembrance of the place. Then, for no particular reason, I went on to tell him about our lovely ghost, always waiting at the head of the stairs, smiling, as if in readiness to greet someone.

"Suddenly, old Elmer's eyes grew brighter, and he straightened up in his chair. A slow smile played around his mouth. Finally, and with some effort, he spoke:

167

" 'Yes,' he murmured. 'I knew her well. Fact is, I *was engaged to her once.*'

"There was something about the way he said it that stopped me from asking any more questions. But later, I saw Gus on one of his weekly trips to the general store, and I told him what Elmer had said. Gus confirmed the story.

"The pretty girl who lived in my house, Gus said, was the only woman Elmer had ever loved. But it was all so long ago, and Gus couldn't remember her name.

"I don't know whatever put the idea into Max Anderson's head to have the hero of his play fall in love with a ghost," Mrs. Dixon concluded, "but that's no more mysterious than the fact that our ghost hasn't been seen once at the head of the stairs since old Elmer died."

A year or so later, after I too had become a neighbor in Rockland County, I told Maxwell Anderson the story.

"A fascinating yarn," was his comment. "Oddly enough, I had never heard a word of it when I decided to write that play."

MY OWN GHOST STORY

Do I have a ghost story of my own? *Do I!*

I will have to preface it by saying, like everyone else, no, I don't *believe* in haunted houses; all I know is that I *own* one.

As a matter of fact, I have owned a couple of haunted houses, and am probably the only man living who built a third house to get away from two spook-riddled habitats!

The first one was a most unlikely place to harbor a ghost. It was a shingled cottage on Long Island Sound, at Groton Long Point, Connecticut, to be exact. Though the fact that it was haunted wasn't made apparent to me directly, I knew all the people and the circumstances involved, and I know that the story is true as gospel.

Like Dorothy Massey, I eschew ghost stories that are "corny"; those dealing with such time-worn phenomena as mysterious ladies in white, clanking chains, et cetera. We both like our ghost stories down to earth, so to speak —and if an interrupted session of dish-washing doesn't fit that category, what does?

Groton Long Point is a rather charming little summer resort, occupied almost entirely during the summer months by families from Connecticut, New York and New Jersey. In the wintertime it is almost completely deserted. I had spent several pleasant week ends there at a tiny inn operated by a retired vaudeville actress and decided that it offered such a pleasant change from New York City during the hot months that I would become a summer resident myself.

The house I did buy was owned by the innkeeper next door, the aforesaid actress, who used it as a private residence for herself and her elderly mother, and as an overflow guest house.

My first gesture was to remove the name of the place—

169

the sort of name that some people wish on their summer houses, Solid Kumfurt. (Imagine any respectable ghost putting up with that!)

I never got much use out of the place, as about this time the United States became involved in World War II and gasoline rationing made such lengthy week-end trips from New York both expensive and impractical. So, when cold weather arrived, I offered the house as a winter residence to a friend, Miss Elsie Raymond, who had a clerical job in New London and wasn't averse to commuting the eleven miles to Groton Long Point in order to enjoy a pleasant and comfortable home.

Miss Raymond was in all ways a practical and courageous woman. She could drive a car, steer a boat and handle a gun with equal assurance—as well as stoke a furnace —and I knew that she could take care of both herself and the house in any emergency. However, since the Point is almost completely deserted in winter, I did have some slight qualms about her spending the long winter months in the house, alone but for an aged white cat. As it turned out, she apparently wasn't entirely alone. . . .

On my first visit to the place the following spring, I asked Miss Raymond how she had fared during the winter, specifically, if she had been disturbed at any time, meaning by prowlers.

"I was, once," Miss R. replied, meditatively, "and perhaps he *was* a prowler.

"It was back in December, when the days were growing shorter. By the time I had driven back to the house from New London, it was already dark. On this particular night, I didn't get home until about 5:30 P.M. The fog had changed into an icy drizzle and a stiff land breeze was bringing freezing weather.

"I fixed myself a tray supper and took it into the living room, to eat beside a wood fire. After that, I washed the dishes and was about to empty the dishwater down the drain, when it occurred to me that the pipes might freeze in the night—and you know what a disaster it can be when pipes burst in the country. So I decided to empty the dishwater outside, on the back road. By now the wind had risen almost to a gale.

"Both of my hands were busy holding the dishpan, but I managed to turn the doorknob and was trying to balance the dishpan and wangle the door open with one foot when the door suddenly blew open of its own accord and a man breezed in, almost as if blown by the wind.

"He had piercing black eyes, and he glared at me as if he resented being kept outside. But when he stopped under the kitchen light, for a split second, his expression changed, almost to one of friendliness. He was wearing a lumber jacket, such as they wear around the country here, with the collar turned up, and a felt hat that had been trimmed around the edges in scallops.

"I put the dishpan on the stove and started to bolt for the door, but when I turned around, the man was gone. By this time I wasn't so frightened as I was hopping mad at the intrusion.

"The stranger hadn't had time even to get into the living room, but I went in there, looking for him. He wasn't there. Then I got my gun and went into every room in the house, upstairs and down. I even searched the cellar, but the man wasn't there, either. As the saying goes, he had vanished into thin air.

"The whole thing took place in a matter of seconds, almost, but I remembered every detail of the man's appearance, and especially his clothes."

At this point, with my hair practically standing on end, I managed to ask Miss Raymond if there had been any follow-up to this experience.

"Yes," Miss R. answered. "When Marie [the actress from whom I bought the house] and her mother returned from Florida, where they had spent most of the winter, I told them about it. Marie laughed, a trifle nervously, and scoffed at the whole business; said I must have been drinking 'the wrong brand of scotch' that evening. But when she left the room, her mother continued to sit there, and I saw that tears were streaming down her face.

" 'Don't pay any attention to Marie,' the old lady said. 'I know what you're talking about. That man was *my son*. I recognized him by your description, particularly your description of his clothes. Those clothes are in a trunk up in the attic next door.'

"The old lady then went on to describe her son, and her description of him dovetailed exactly with my memory of the strange man. Her son, Marie's brother, had spent a lot of time in this house and he loved the place. He had been gassed in France during World War I and developed lung trouble. When he left here, he went directly to a veterans' hospital, where he died."

Shortly after this, Miss Raymond's business took her elsewhere, and I rented the house to a Navy lieutenant who was stationed at the nearby Submarine Base. His wife was delighted with the place, but shortly after moving in she made an odd request. Would I, she wrote, kindly buy a Venetian blind for the front door?

"I am a timid Navy wife," her letter read, "often alone at night, and I would appreciate this small protection from the Peeping Toms and bogeymen of Groton Long Point."

I am sure my new tenant had never heard of Miss Raymond's experience with the mysterious visitor, and the request wasn't very logical, since the front door was well protected by a ten-foot, screened-in porch. But I decided that if I wanted to keep my tenant I had better supply the Venetian blind and ask no further questions.

When wartime conditions made the trips to New London and Groton Long Point too difficult, I sold the beach house and bought a place in Rockland County, up the west side of the Hudson, about an hour's drive from New York City.

Just what attracted me to that particular house will ever remain a mystery, for in its rundown condition it suggested a Charles Addams version of an Early American ruin. Knowing more about old houses now than I did then, it is more likely that it was *I* who attracted the house, and it was I that was being *taken over!*

I first saw the place on a bleak March day, when the wind was howling down out of the Ramapo Mountains like a Sabbath of witches, and the little house seemed to shiver and shake in the cold March wind like an old street beggar that has known better days.

There were no warning signs saying "Watch Your Step —*Haunted House!*"

I knew nothing of the history of the place, beyond the fact that during Prohibition times, moonshiners had operated there; that it dated from pre-Revolutionary times, and that its location, Camp Hill, got that name because

Mad Anthony Wayne was supposed to have bivouacked his troops there, before or after the famous battle of Stony Point.

Restored, it became a cozy and delightful little dwelling. But I soon learned that I had made it warm and comfortable for others besides myself. . . .

During the restoration period, I had managed to spend quite a few nights there alone, when the strange noises that occurred might have been ascribed—to borrow a line from Alexander Woollcott—to "the antiphonal creaking of a shutter in the night wind." Oddly enough, it was only after electricity had been installed, and vacuum cleaners, garbage disposals, and other modern appurtenances brought in that mysterious "things" began to happen.

"I have an odd feeling," I remarked more than once, "that someone wants very much to get *into* this house," and on one occasion amplified this remark by saying, "I was startled out of a sound sleep the other day by a loud banging from the iron door-knocker. My imagination, of course," I added, rather self-deprecatingly; "there was no one at the door."

There was no one at the door again, when the same thing occurred on a November evening. This time, a friend answered my door, and was understandably baffled to find no one outside.

My houseman found a similar experience enough of an excuse never to spend another night there alone. On that occasion, I had occupied the guest house and came in for breakfast in what we called the "main house," to face a very sullen servant.

"The guest house (which I had just restored) is a nice place in which to spend the night," I announced cheerily.

"This house would be a nice place to spend the night," he muttered, "if *they'd let you alone.* I got up three times in the night to answer the front door. I thought you had changed your mind and decided to sleep here."

A workman engaged to paint the kitchen was the next person to complain.

"Every afternoon they walk up the stairs, about four o'clock," he growled.

"*They*—?" I inquired.

"Somebody—somebody with boots on."

A sophisticated lady guest who spent two nights in the

173

upstairs bedroom later thanked me for my hospitality but asked that I not repeat the invitation. "I simply couldn't take it again," she remarked. "That bedroom was the busiest place I ever spent a night in."

Following a gay dinner party in the Early American kitchen, one slightly pixillated young woman excused herself and presumably went upstairs to sleep it off. A few moments later, there was a terrific thud from upstairs.

"Better go upstairs and look after Eloise," one of the other women guests remarked. "She's probably fallen off the couch."

But on investigation, the young woman was discovered sitting by the fire in the downstairs sitting room, quietly reading. There was *no one* in the bedroom upstairs!

About this time, we began to notice mysterious dents on the pewter, much of which had come into the house in perfect condition. One water pitcher had five distinct indentations—four on one side, one on the other—and it gave us quite a turn when one male guest with unusually large hands fitted his four fingers and thumb into them.

Even more bewildering was an incident involving a pane of glass in my front door (again, the front door)! The glass for some time had been cracked, and I knew that eventually it would have to be replaced. When a second crack appeared, for no reason at all, I became afraid that a good slam of the door would scatter glass, either inside the hall, or outside the door on the porch.

The glass did fall out eventually, but when it happened I was not in the house. Guests were spending the week end there and, again, I had resorted to the guest house. When I came up to the main house for breakfast, I found the glass gone—but *there were no signs of glass splinters either inside or outside the front door!*

My guests were still sleeping, so I waited until they were up, and then I asked if either one of them had had occasion to open the front door in the night, or to give their dog an airing in the morning. They assured me that they had not opened the front door for *any* reason.

Now if anyone had been playing a practical joke on me —something that inevitably crossed my mind—they would most assuredly have left the glass fragments in some place where I would be likely to find them—on the kitchen table, the ice box, or some other prominent spot. But there was no trace of the glass fragments anywhere, and the mystery continued to deepen.

The week before this happened, while on one of my brief visits to the house—as a Broadway columnist, I am obliged to *live* in New York City, with whatever time out I can spare for the country—I had been working on a wire extension for an electric clock that rested on a shelf over the kitchen fireplace. This shelf was actually a plate rail that extended halfway around the room, a good eight feet above the floor. To bore a hole in this shelf to admit an electric wire, it was necessary to stand on a small ladder or a chair.

I had been too pressed for time to finish the job on my first try, and was too occupied looking after guests the following week end to complete it, so I did not resume the project until the Wednesday following.

When I mounted the ladder this second time, I discovered, to my intense astonishment, the missing fragments of glass from the front hall door, lying on the plate rail!

This sort of prank, I knew by now, is the sort of thing usually blamed on a *poltergeist*. No, I kept saying to myself, it *couldn't* happen *here*. But it *did!*

Word of these phenomena eventually reached the ears of an internationally known psychic, Mrs. Eileen Garrett. I was invited to call on the lady at her Madison Avenue apartment, and she told me that she had had some success in de-haunting houses in England, but never in this country.

"Please invite me up to your place sometime," she asked smilingly, "and I will see what I can discover."

After the necessary preliminary arrangements had been made, Mrs. Garrett arrived on a Saturday afternoon, with quite an entourage. With her was her secretary, a young woman; a psychiatrist with a distinguished name; a Viennese "physicist"; a photographer equipped with an infrared camera; and a magazine writer, who brought along a tape-recording machine.

Mrs. Garrett looked the place over; a very brief tour, considering the size of the place—living room, hall, and kitchen downstairs, and a master bedroom above. She quickly concluded that the upstairs bedroom was the haunted spot. While the others were still downstairs, she gave me her brief impression of the background of the

175

house. The road in front of the house, she said, had once "gone on" (it *did* once "go on," up into the Ramapo Mountains, where George Washington is said to have concealed his horses, to keep the British from finding them). There was once a "wagon way" at the foot of the hill (this I located weeks later). There had been a partition in the room, which had been used for storing grain, apples, etc. (I had personally taken down this partition.) Mrs. Garrett also "got the feeling" that someone, acting as a lookout, had once sat by the upstairs window, with a rifle over his knee. And this was exactly what had happened during the moonshiner days!

By now I was convinced that Mrs. Garrett was at least on the beam and I was prepared to listen respectfully to whatever else she was about to reveal.

She then called the other members of the party upstairs, seated herself in an Early American rocker and declared that she was ready to go to work, or, as she put it, go into "full trance."

Surrounded by the above mentioned people, all there to observe or take notes, Mrs. Garrett then proceeded to pass out completely, in what appeared to be a catalyptic state. Though her eyes were open throughout, they were rolled upward and appeared to be sightless.

Soon from her lips came mutterings, in a deep, masculine voice. Mrs. Garrett's secretary then confided to me that this was Uvani, Mrs. Garrett's East Indian guide, who apparently was in command of excellent, pedantic English.

After a long, one-sided dissertation from Uvani, which I took to be a sort of warming-up process, another personality came through, and then things really began to happen. Let the magazine writer's story, compiled from the stenographer's notes and the tape recording, take it from here:

"Slowly, the new personality working through Madam's body—obviously a man—sat up; his hands violently vibrating, as if in palsy; his face distorted in extreme pain; his eyes blinking, then staring at us with no sign of recognition. This was accompanied by increasingly inarticulate outcries and deeply emotional weeping.

"For a minute or two, the new personality maintained his position in the chair, then suddenly leaned over and crashed to the floor . . . one leg continuing

176

to execute rapid, convulsive movements . . . the leg obviously had been badly damaged. Now and then, the subject would throw his hand to his head, touching it as if to indicate that he was in great pain, there, too . . ."

What transpired before our startled eyes in the upstairs bedroom of my farmhouse on that Saturday afternoon would make a scenario for a Kenneth Roberts novel of Revolutionary times. Mrs. Garrett lay prone at my feet, sobbing convulsively and babbling in broken English. In pantomime, she seemed to be attempting to draw an imaginary map, the gestures suggesting the use of a quill pen.

The story, as it thus emerged, concerned a Polish (not Hessian) mercenary who had been trapped in some machination between the pro-American French and the anti-American British troops involved in the Revolutionary War. He had been chased into the house by the "big men" —apparently British soldiers—and horribly beaten. His teeth knocked out (this illustrated by a grisly pantomime), his head bashed in and one leg broken, he had been left there to die. He didn't die—then—but lived on for many pain-wracked days, broken in mind as well as body. And this was the spirit who was haunting my house!

At long last, the East Indian guide, Uvani, again took over, and speaking through the medium, in his calm and cultured English, explained that the spirit of Andreas (or Litch, the nickname by which the Polish mercenary was known to his soldier pals) was set at rest, and would never disturb my house again.

The séance had taken a full hour. Mrs. Garrett came out of it as if awakening from pleasant slumber and asked to be told, step by step, what had taken place during her trance. I concluded that she was either the greatest living actress outside the theater, or that she was genuinely possessed. And since Mrs. Garrett is known as a woman of both intellect and integrity, neither her honesty nor her sincerity could be questioned.

She herself was convinced that the de-haunting had been a complete success, and assured me that peace thereafter would reign in my troubled house. Perhaps; I haven't yet mustered up enough courage to put it to the test and spend other nights there, alone.

Did the melodrama enacted for us on that Saturday afternoon explain the frantic rappings at the front door . . . the sound of heavy boots on the stairs . . . the thud of a body falling in the room above . . . or the dozens of other manifestations that neither I nor anyone else was ever able to explain?

I don't know. What I do know is that I find the old wagon shed that I have converted into a studio (my "third house") a far pleasanter and more peaceful place in which to spend my nights and days. . . .

Well, these are some of the stories I've heard. Maybe you do believe them, maybe you don't—at any rate, I hope they've entertained you. And maybe they've made you stop for a minute and think about the world we take so much for granted.

As I said before, these are just a few of the many stories told me. If anyone reading this book has had similar experiences, I would be delighted to hear them. I can be reached by letter in care of my publisher. And maybe sometime later, we can have more Spooks—Deluxe or otherwise.

INDEX

184

186

ABOUT THE AUTHOR:

Danton Walker goes everywhere, knows everybody. As a Broadway columnist—described in a Time write-up as "Mr. Two Million Circulation"—his beat is primarily the theatres, cafes and all the glittering night life for which New York is famous. Hardly the life, you'd say, in which the supernatural would have much chance to pervade. Yet, in the course of interviewing a great many people—sophisticated, intelligent professional people —Danton Walker discovered that nearly every one of them had a ghost story—his own ghost story! Oh, no: none of them believed that such things happen; all they know is that they did happen, and to them!

Georgia-born, Danton Walker dates his interest in supernatural goings-on from about the age of six, while listening breathlessly to the endless series of superb spook stories told him by his old nurse. After World War I he traveled extensively in Europe as a member of Herbert Hoover's American Relief Administration and one of his discoveries in the Carpathian mountains—the Dracula country of Hungary—was that there werewolves are not confined to the pages of books.

Back in this country, he resumed the career he had planned before the war and became successively a dancer, actor and writer on the theatre. Eventually, in order to eat regularly, he recalls, he took the post of secretary to the famous drama critic, Alexander Woollcott, which he counts one of his most interesting experiences. And Woollcott, he soon discovered, was one of the best ghost-story tellers of his time!

Stints on The Billboard and The New Yorker eventually led to his present one with The New York Daily News, the tabloid with the largest circulation in America, where his first position was, oddly, assistant to the financial editor. Eventually, he worked his way back into the music, drama, movie, radio and night club life and wound up writing his Broadway column, which wraps them all up.

Danton Walker's favorite hobby—next to collecting ghost stories—is travel, and his vacations have taken him to such exotic spots as Peru, Alaska, Morocco, to Rio de Janeiro, Havana, Mexico City and other South and Central American cities, as well as the great capitals of Europe. And one of the things he learned on these travels is that the supernatural has no geography.

Mr. Walker has not only hobnobbed with the famous; he has also hobnobbed with the hobgoblins of the famous. And here they are.